JESUS:
God and Man

Larry Mullins

JESUS: GOD and MAN
by LARRY MULLINS
Illustrated by the Author

© COPYRIGHT 1977 Larry Mullins
© COPYRIGHT 2011 Larry Mullins, St. Augustine, Florida

SECOND PRINTING

All rights reserved.

CreateSpace
A Division of Amazon, Inc.

Jesus: God and Man is based upon revelatory information from *The Urantia Book.* Our book, *Jesus: God and Man,* does not contend with the Biblical gospels, but rather expands and enhances their presentation of the life and teachings of Jesus. The role of revelation is not to establish a new religion. It is rather to sweep away the logic-tight barriers between religion, science and philosophy: *"Reason is the proof of science, faith the proof of religion, logic the proof of philosophy, but revelation is validated only by human experience. Science yields knowledge; religion yields happiness; philosophy yields unity; revelation confirms the experiential harmony of this triune approach to universal reality."* [The Urantia Book, page 1106, par. 7] Some readers may consider this expanded treatment of the bestowal of Jesus in such a cosmic context as entertaining science fiction rather than revelation. However, our mission is to inspire a new generation of believers to truly "follow after" the Master in the demonstration of his authentic life of religious devotion to the doing of God's will and of his consecration to the unselfish service of humankind.

Library of Congress
Catalogue Card Number:
77-93275

www.Jesus-GodandMan.com

To BERKELEY ELLIOTT
1917 - 1995

Without Berkeley and the members of the
First Urantia Society of Oklahoma
this historic project would never
have happened.

JESUS:
God and Man

INTRODUCTION
to the Second Edition of
Jesus: God and Man

IN 1976 I MET BERKELEY ELLIOTT IN TULSA, Oklahoma at a study group for *The Urantia Book*. When Berkeley learned that I am a writer, she suggested that I might be able to help her with a special project. I had no idea that the project would virtually consume my life for the next year.

The Urantia Book is a tome of 2097 pages. About one-third of the book is devoted to the life and teachings of Jesus of Nazareth. *The Urantia Book* is soundly grounded in the historical facts of the New Testament, yet it enlarges upon the Biblical information, and places Jesus in a bold new cosmic perspective. Berkeley explained that she wanted to develop a multimedia production about Jesus based upon *The Urantia Book*. All she had produced so far was the working title, "*Jesus: God and Man.*" She told me Urantia Foundation had agreed to permit her to make this multimedia. (At that time Urantia Foundation was the owner of the copyright of *The Urantia Book.**) However, the Foundation insisted that she could not use any direct quotes from *The Urantia Book* itself. Berkeley asked if I could "dash off a few pages" of script for her toward the purpose of creating a derivative work.

The "few pages" became the book that is now in your hands. *Jesus: God and Man* was well received as a multimedia, and the Oklahoma study group decided they wanted to print the script in book form. For more than two decades, Urantia Foundation had zealously guarded *The Urantia Book's* copyright and had refused to grant permission for any secondary works. However, after a period of scrutiny of the manuscript of *Jesus: God and Man* by several leading Urantians, the Trustees of Urantia Foundation granted permission for the private publication of 1,000 copies of the book *Jesus: God and Man.*

The 1,000 copies soon sold out. So it was that very few new Urantia Book readers have ever heard of *Jesus: God and Man.* Once in a while a used copy appears on Amazon, usually priced at $150 or more.

Jesus: God and Man was the first derivative work ever permitted by Urantia Foundation. I hope you find it of interest. Thanks to modern technology readers can have an exact replica of the book's original contents.

Larry Mullins
St. Augustine, Florida

---

*The Urantia Book is now in the public domain.

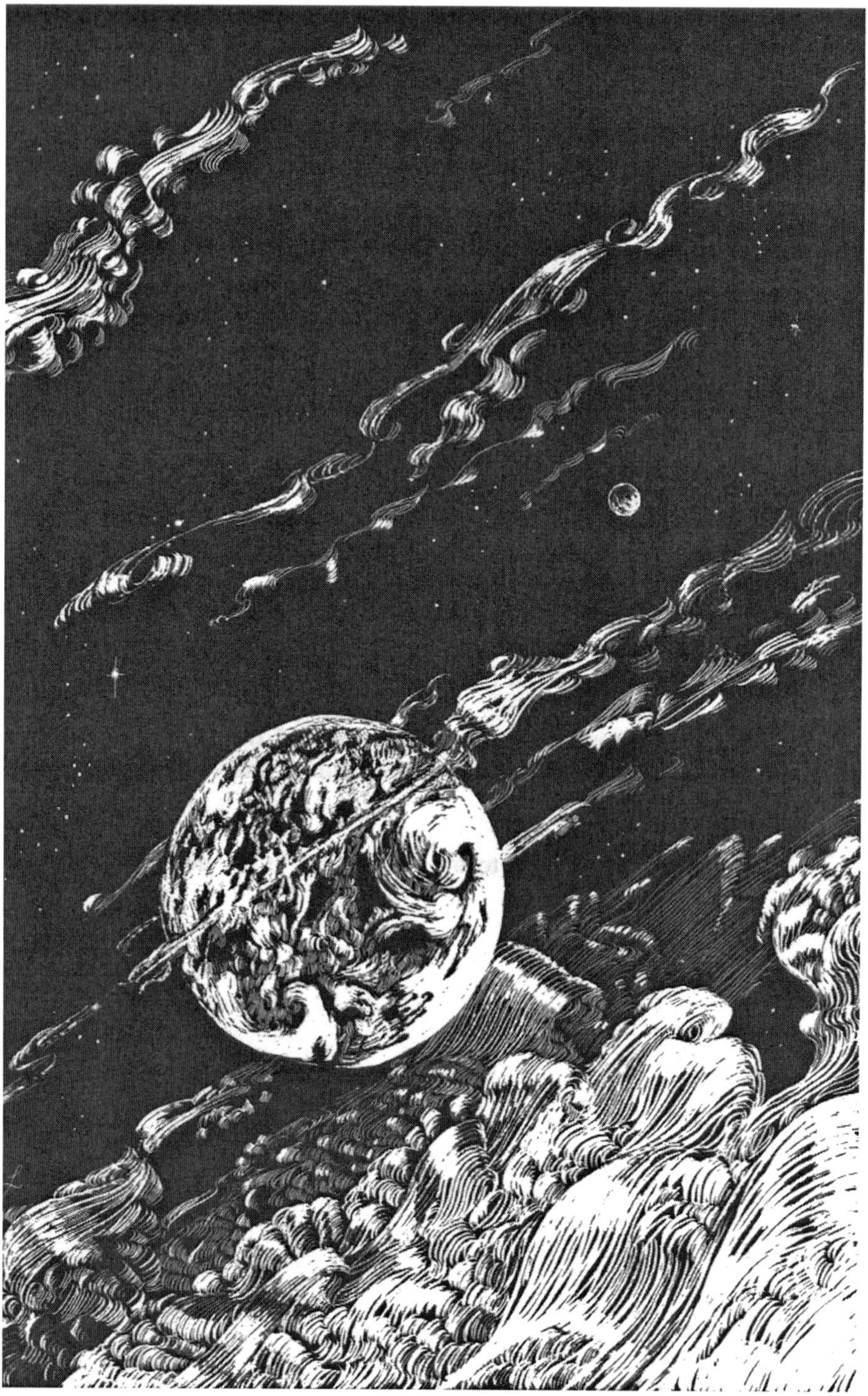

JESUS:
God and Man

I

"...one of these bits of cosmic dust..."

THE ETERNAL FATHER SPOKE . . .

    thus confirming
    the everlasting union
    of Creator Son and Creative Spirit.

SO IT WAS
    that the love of the Eternal Father
        richly blended with the mercy of the Eternal Son
            was focalized in Michael,
            and complemented by the modulating power
            of the Eternal Mother.

Liberated now
        from Paradise obligations
        our beloved Michael and our Mother Spirit
            took leave of the Eternal Core of Perfection

                400 billion years ago.

Past an endless panorama of swirling universes
        traveled Michael and his consort
            on their stupendous evolutionary enterprise:

            To recreate
            from grossest physical matter
            and rawest energy
            The Eternal Pattern of Perfection,
                and to manifest
                in time and space
                    the awesome attributes
                    of God the Sevenfold.

ON AND ON they traveled
    to the outermost periphery
        of the Seventh Superuniverse –
        near the dead vaults of space –
        to a disintegrating
        monarch of light,
            the enormous nebula
                Andronover.

    There began our universe.

        And they called it: Nebadon.

POISED AND READY
    mobilizing gigantic space energies
    the power directors awaited
    the supreme creative catalyst.

And when Michael's companion Mother Spirit
    permeated all of Nebadon-to-be
        the power centers and physical controllers
        swung into action of
            grandest magnitude.

        First came the formation
        of the Architectural Sphere of Salvington
            that imposing nucleus
            of one hundred headquarter
            clusters of constellations,
                and ten thousand auxiliary
                Architectural Worlds,
                and one hundred
                      times one hundred
                      times one thousand
                      evolutionary worlds.

SO MICHAEL of Nebadon's Universe was born: Unique
                                                            diverse
                                                            exclusive
                                                            and original.

IN TIME the invisible scale
   of power and matter leveled
      and the universe acquired
      a kind of equilibrium.

   Then came forth
   from the creative conception
   of Michael and the Mother Spirit
      the singular personification
      of divinity's ideal and character:

      Gabriel . . .

      The Bright and Morning Star
      The Supreme Administrator
      The first of a vast array
      of Universe Sons and Daughters.

FAR FROM the nucleus of activity
    on the remote fringes
        of Michael's vast creative adventure
            6 billion years ago
                our sun was born. . .

An isolated
    unimposing spark
        among the galaxies of
            dazzling, mammoth orbs.

THE SUN was a solitary sentinel
    for a billion years
        until the last Architectural Sphere was completed.

MEANWHILE,
    inexorably, steadily, ponderously,
        an immensely powerful
            dark giant of space
                approached our sun.

Core of the Angona System
    this monster of darkness
    took half a billion years
    to finally lock into a titanic
    gravitational struggle
    with our mother star.

In a prodigious series of convulsions
        the sun surrendered vast portions of herself
        so that a new solar system was born.

Unwittingly
    one of these bits of cosmic dust
    was destined to be the stage
    for one of the most monumental
        universe dramas ever enacted
        in all of creation.

But that was in the distant future.

THE COOLING Urantian embryo
   would circle mother sun
      four billion times
         before it was ready to receive
           even the first seeds of life.

Meanwhile
howling winds swept back and forth
across the desolate oceans
and tore at the rocky shores of the
      drifting, barren continents.

Yet slowly —
imperceptibly —
Urantia was being prepared for the miracle of life.

Five hundred and fifty million years ago
in the warm waters of three sheltered bays
the architects and bearers of life
planted the precious treasures.

And these sculptors and guardians of living matter
    would toil ceaselessly
        to keep the wonder alive.

So it was that valiantly, tenuously, life began on Urantia.

As TIME passed the microbic beginnings
　　unfolded into a wonderful panorama
　　　　of evolving, struggling, upreaching
　　　　　　living matter.

Some life forms
vanished in agony
　　while others,
　　　　as tenacious as the wild elements,
　　　　　　　　emerged triumphant.
The natural shifting and selection continued
　　from crude lichen and moss
　　to tiny creatures
　　　　that swam in the warm green seas
　　　　　　insulated from the pitiless elements.

Plants, first feeble and puny,
　　began to wax into luxurious foliage
　　　　and fern trees rose proudly in the brooding sky.
A few enterprising creatures
　　　　dared forsake the protective womb of the sea
　　　　　　and ventured onto land.

NEW sounds were heard
    as lumbering beasts
    and giant insects
    and hissing reptiles
        laid claim to the Urantian paradise.
  Even the trackless, pristine air was startled
    as amazing birdlike creatures
        transcended the territorial contest below.

THE MOON watched in silver wonder
    as for millions of years
        its mist-shrouded neighbor
          hosted the pageant of evolution.

THEN it came to pass
    in those dark thick forests
    where echoed the tigers roar
    and the scream of circling birds of prey
  that a new creature
      timid, curious, and intelligent
        began to venture
          from its tree sanctuaries
            and scamper over rotting logs
            and steaming grass
            in an incessant search
            for food.

IT WAS much later
    that a silent sigh of pleasure
      passed through the Life Carriers:
          One of these primate creatures gave birth
            to the twins Andon and Fonta.
            These, our remotest ancestors,
            were brought forth wailing and kicking
            into an incredibly lonely world.
        Unseen celestial beings hovered near
        their thin and terrified bodies
          watching, waiting.

S O desolate and dangerous was life
    among the primeval tribe!
        And when their mother fell
            under the onslaught of gibbon's fangs
                Andon and Fonta decided to flee.

        As they plunged northward
        the Universe took note
        of their monumental resolution
        and the history of humankind began.
The tribe noted briefly their absence
    watched the grief-sick father wander off to die
        and then turned their savage eyes away
            to look for food.

THE descendents of Andon and Fonta
    emerged in growing numbers.
    They shivered in the rain
    They endured the burning sun
    They survived the curse of the ice
        and they struggled on.

More and more man's dark mind was encouraged
    by the flickering down-grasping
        love of God
        and many were indwelt
        with a fragment of immortality.

Yet man lived in incessant danger.
    From every side his right to live was challenged.
        The merciless elements
        the bloodthirsty beasts
        and worst of all
            his own brother tribes
            very nearly snuffed out
                the precious torch of humanity.

MAN, surrounded by endless cycles of life and death . . .
   Man —
      the potential Son of God
         began to build and create.
         He began to hear friendly sounds
            from his children's lips
      and in the clear sunlight
         he perceived rich colors
            where all had been dark and grey before.

Another evolutionary milestone was passed
      as families formed.
         Man huddled in these families —
         families huddled in tribes —
         until there were longer and longer intervals
            without hunger or danger.

Man
seeking to insure his good estate, worshiped.
      He worshiped animals, for they were food
            the elements, for he feared them
            the heavens, for they
                were incomprehensible.

And man found these gods fickle and demanding.

THEN NEW gods came, 500 thousand years ago.
    To primitive man
        Caligastia and his hundredfold staff
            were god-men, indeed.
                Caligastia, brilliant, trained and dedicated,
                    became the Planetary Prince
                    of Urantia.

Myths would declare that gods from heaven
                    walked the earth in those days.
    These giants of skill and intellect
    were eager to accelerate the progress
    of the six emerging races.

The uplift was
    steady and impressive.
    For three hundred thousand years
    man enjoyed enrichment from the masterful expertise
        of Caligastia and the One Hundred.

BUT, far away from the struggling little planet

       an incredibly wanton and destructive concept had been conceived and was being nurtured in the vainglorious mind
                    of Lucifer.

LUCIFER! Son of morning
        prodigious of intellect
        distinguished of career
        splendid system sovereign.

LUCIFER! He began to weave his plans
    with nefarious threads of logic
  spinning a web of delusion
  that would ensnare a host of hapless creatures,
        trusting creatures,
        allured by truthful trifles
        to be betrayed
        in the deepest consequence.
  So many would fall
      hopelessly entangled
        in the warp and woof
          of Lucifer's deceit.

So many would slip
    farther and farther
      from light of truth
        eventually to submerge with Lucifer
          into that abyss of darkness —

              cosmic insanity.

WITH stunning effrontery and caustic clarity
 Lucifer's narcissistic manifesto
  echoed over the sea of glass of Satania
   two hundred thousand years ago.

Chaos followed
 seeming to validate
  Lucifer's power and invulnerability.
It was in this atmosphere
 of upheaval, uncertainty
  and grotesque license
that Lucifer's lieutenant, Satan,
 won Caligastia
  to the suicidal cause.
Our planetary prince
 in a cynical betrayal of his trust
  cast his lot with Lucifer.
Caligastia's tremendous prestige
 gave considerable weight
  to the side of darkness.
The poison was contagious
 infecting hosts of subordinates.

THOSE loyal and steadfast
 clustered around Van and Amadon
  in defiance of the evil powers
   being marshalled against them.
    But Van's reassuring message of support
     was marooned somewhere in space
      between Urantia and Edentia
       when the spiritual circuits
        were severed.

Thus isolated
 Urantia hurled through space
  and plunged into the darkness
   of celestial quarantine.

    The planet seemed lost indeed.

THE flame of truth flickered dangerously
    in the winds of unbridled, egoistic license.

Faithful souls
though spiritually adrift
remained true to Michael's cause
and groped for a celestial hand.
Although the Melchizedek Twelve came to help
    the heroic Van and Amadon salvage what they could
        the tides of unchecked barbarism
            swept away virtually all of man's progress . . .

        and left him socially fragmented
        and culturally impoverished.

THE rebellion was madness,
　　it was destined to fail.

　　The Son of God
　　　　would one day
　　　　　　strip away the rotten scaffolding
　　　　　　　of the leaders' authority
　　　　　　and they would collapse and fall ignominiously.

　　　　　　Their followers yet unrepentant
　　　　　　　　now without an axis
　　　　　　　　would be dispersed like leaves
　　　　　　　　as though by some divine wind.

　　　　　　Justice, slow and sure
　　　　　　　　would seal their fates.

Caligastia's once proud headquarters
　　would be ravaged by semi-savage tribes
　　　　as though in vengeance for being misled,
　　　　　　and then would be submerged by a giant tidal wave
　　　　　　as though to be cleansed
　　　　　　　　of the final evidence
　　　　　　　　　of Caligastia's
　　　　　　　　　　abortive mission.

DEPRIVED of his birthright
    contaminated by the gospel of darkness
    man's beast-like nature was now augmented
    with an intelligence unmodulated by moral law
    and he became more savage
    than any natural beast.

Man lost his way.

THERE was a single enclave of hope
in this ocean of dangerous darkness.

Eden.

In Eden the faithful waited
and prepared to receive the promised help.

In this splendid Garden of Anticipation and Belief
man created a sanctuary worthy of gods
                                   and waited.

The vigil ended 37 thousand years ago.

Whispered legends would one day
    tribute the arrival
        of two new creatures
           and men would call them Adam and Eve.

ADAM and Eve —
 immortal, celestial, wonderful,
  came to cleanse the stagnant gene-pool of man
   so depleted and exhausted.

With this revitalization
 the evolutionary stream
  would flow again,
   cleansed, enriched and vital.

Songs of rejoicing
 filled the perfumed air of Eden
  and hope for Urantia dawned anew.

 The torch was passed.

 The Urantian trust was transferred
  from the Melchizedeks
   to Adam and Eve
    and the wondrous pair
     was left alone.

 An unbearable cosmic loneliness descended.

WHO CAN judge
    which was more tragic?

        Caligastia's premeditated betrayal
            or Eve's impatience for good?

Eve, in her well-intended innocence
    fatally amended the divine mandate
        and broke the sacred trust.

Adam, with touching compassion and love
    chose to follow the misguided example of his beloved
        so that he could share her fate
            and not be left alone on such a planet!

        The hope for Urantia sank
        even as the glorious garden
        submerged slowly, silently
        into the shimmering
        Mediterranean.

GUILT
   weighed heavily on the hearts
      of Adam and Eve.

   Surely this was the fatal blow
   for this ill-starred planet!

   The ever merciful Michael
   soothed their tortured minds
   with this divine hint:

   Urantia,
     the pathetic orphan of Nebadon
        so culturally
           and physically
              and spiritually deprived,
                 would be the host
                 for the final bestowal
                 of the Creator Son himself!

MICHAEL'S wondrous decision
    astonished the celestial hosts of heaven.

    Six times successful
        this Light of the Living God
            the Personality of the Eternal Father
                and the Mercy of the Eternal Son
                    would now shine as a beacon
                        against the foil of dark Urantia!

For so it is that Creator Sons
    can best understand the afflictions
        of the struggling bits of divinity
            that they so lovingly create.

AND YET –

    Urantia – a planet
    with such a poverty of enlightenment,
    was this not unredeemably fallow soil?

    Would even a Creator Son,
    with his immense grace and power
    not find Urantia bankrupt of hope?

And so Machiventa Melchizedek came.

    He came to prepare the way,
    to pour spiritual waters
    on the arid Urantian hearts.

AND Machiventa Melchizedek labored wisely.
    Resolute to his single mission
  his ministry was a blessing to all mankind.
    Abraham counseled with him
        and his faith was consecrated
            by Melchizedek's wisdom.
  The winds of renewed hope
      scattered seeds of truth to all civilization . . .
  to the lands of the Sphinx and past the Ganges
  past the cloud-capped Himalayas
  to the land of the yellow men
  and through the tribes of Europe
  and across the turbulent channel waters
  to the savages of Britain.

  And these seeds took root and bore living fruit.

Melchizedek toiled
    for nearly one hundred years
    and then left as mysteriously as he had come.

      His truths were passed
       from prophet to prophet
      and sage to sage
      while Urantia awaited
           the promised Son of God.

A HUSH descended over Nebadon.
 The seventh bestowal promised to be
  the ultimate adventure
   for their beloved creator.
  This time Michael would contest the darkness
  of human ignorance and fear,
  a blackness more terrible
  more utterly desolate
  than the vacuous
  chambers of space.

  Michael's resolve
  was to endure the agony of human existence
  and to conquer forever
  the illusion of
  personality
  isolation.

To this end Michael of Nebadon
   would live in light and life
   as Jesus of Nazareth,
   Christ the Supreme,
   the superlative example
    of poise, faith and courage.

SOON MICHAEL would surrender consciousness.
>   He would soon venture into darkness
>   to find his little lamb, Urantia
>   so crippled
>   so lost
>   so in need of him
>   and he would
>   bind her wounds
>   and lead her home.

AND ALTHOUGH
>   in the streets of Jerusalem
>   filthy beggars yet held out their cups
>   with withered hands
>   and the shrill cries of merchants could yet be heard
>   violating the Temple of the Father
>   and ragged children with haunted eyes
>   yet played in the dust
>   a miracle was on the way.

WITH stunning swiftness
>   Urantia would become
>   the most important planet
>   in all of Nebadon.

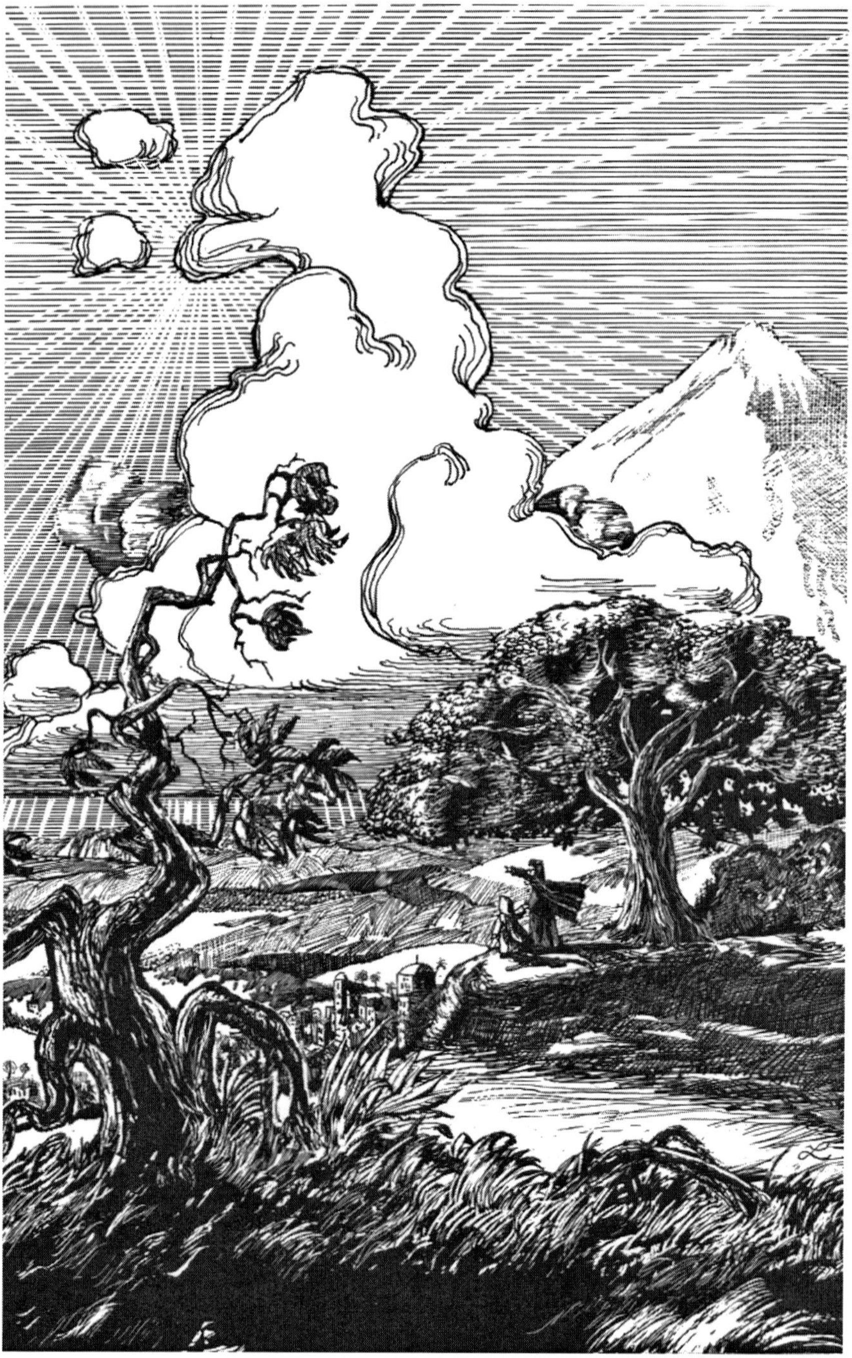

JESUS:
God and Man

II
"...can any good
come out of Nazareth?..."

MICHAEL . . .

 Creator Son of Nebadon,
  removed himself from the sight
  of all of Salvington
   and he was seen no more
    in his accustomed place
     until the seventh bestowal
      had been completed.

SILENT, solemn and eternal
    the towers of Jerusalem
surround the city
    like sixty mighty soldiers.

In the sanctuary of the temple
Zacharias leads the faithful in noontide prayer
    beseeching God
        to send the deliverer of Israel.

At this very moment
    at the home of Zacharias
    in the sun yellowed hills to the west
        a miraculous happening is taking place.

ELIZABETH'S eyes widened
>   as she beheld the dazzling vision of Gabriel —
>   a wondrous angel of light.

And Gabriel spoke to her
>   saying that Elizabeth would bear a son
>   and he would be called John.
>   John would be an ardent man of God
>   who would proclaim and prepare the way
>   for the spiritual liberator of mankind.
>   And her kinswoman Mary
>   would be the mother of the
>   divine teacher, the wonder child.

And then the vision melted into thin air.

Months later Zacharias still frowned with disbelief
>   when he recalled Elizabeth's story.
>   Though his loved wife of many years
>   was indeed with child —
>   could such a miraculous prophecy be genuine?

That night a radiant dream
>   illuminated the mind of Zacharias
>   and his doubts were dispelled.

THE summer had passed
    and the November rains
        had already begun to green the hills
            of Nazareth
                when it was Joseph's time to doubt.

He listened patiently
    as Mary spoke in breathless tones.

    She said that late that afternoon
    their single room dwelling flooded with light.
    There by the low stone table
    stood a splendid celestial being.
    With tender majesty he told Mary
        that she would bear a son
        and he would be called Joshua.
This son would deliver mankind from fear
and would inaugurate the kingdom of heaven on earth.
    And he told her of the mission
    of Elizabeth's child of destiny, John.
    And then the vision dissolved itself into
    the afternoon shadows without a trace.

JOSEPH shook his head incredulously.
   Could such a divine teacher be born of human flesh?

      Soon Joseph had a vision in his sleep
      and a brilliant being told him to be of good faith
      that his son would indeed be a light unto the world.

      Joseph doubted no more.

◦◦◦

WHEN the season of the sun returned
                Mary was heavy with child.

It was time to comply with the decree of Augustus Caesar.
All citizens of the empire must be registered.

   Reconciled
   Joseph smiled as he led the donkey
   laden with his wife and their provisions
   into the tropical valley of the Jordan.
      Mary had prevailed —
      she would accompany him to Bethlehem
         so close to the home of Elizabeth
         her consort mother of light.

They made their way down the valley
     so rich with the tradition of their people.

BY THE third day they prayed
>in the beloved temple at Jerusalem.

>Then they began the steady ascent
>>into the hills where David had tended sheep
>>>to the City of Bethlehem.

The shadows of the olive trees
>stretched long in the afternoon sun
>>when they reached their goal.

But there were no rooms to be had.

There was only a stable
>hewn from rock, coarse and crude,
>but comfortable beyond measure
>to desperate pilgrims with no place to lay their heads.

THE following day
    as the noontide sun peaked high
    in the stainless blue sky
a crystal luminosity enveloped Bethlehem
and silent to mortal ears
celestial seraphim burst into shining hymns of praise.

A refreshing wind blew a mysterious spiritual fragrance
over the lands and waters of Urantia.

Joshua ben Joseph
Jesus the Christ was born.

    Tiny and helpless
    in a cradle-manger
        lay the Creator Son . . .

        The cherished and adored Michael of Nebadon.

MEANWHILE
      men searched for the infant Jesus.

They had traveled from the land of Ur
    a distant place on the banks of the Euphrates
      far beyond the eastern mountains and parched deserts.

These three sages began their westward quest
to find a child of light and life
to be born among the Jews.
    For such was the dream and the vision
    that they had learned of and believed in.

When they found the child at last
    they bent their knees in reverence
    and left gifts to tribute this child of hope and love.

HEROD the Great stroked his beard in frustration.

   For more than a year
         he too had sought the tiny usurper.

         Spies had warned Herod of the mystic birth
             the visit of the priests of Ur
             and the ominous poem of Anna
             that heralded the child as King of the Jews.

         Yet,
         a year later, the danger still existed.

Then Herod hit upon a brilliant plan:
         He would murder all the male children of Bethlehem
             who were not yet two years old!

         And when the macabre butchery was done
         the crown would rest securely on his dark brow.

         So it was that sixteen innocent babies were slain.

AND JESUS?
>   Jesus was gone.
>   Joseph had been warned
>   and had whisked the child away the night before.

Even now
>   safely shrouded in the purple desert night
>   the tiny family was well on the way to Alexandria,
>
> >   the fruitful and flourishing
> >   intellectual mecca
> >   of Urantia.

For two years
>   Mary watched with anxiety
>   as her child of destiny
>   played happily with other children
> >   under the Egyptian sun.

THEN news came:
>   Herod the Great was dead.
>   The family could return home!

JOSEPH, Mary and young Jesus
> at last were sailing toward Joppa.

As the boat stemmed the blue waves of the Mediterranean
> the parents speculated
>> on the future of Joshua ben Joseph.

Would he be,
> as Mary believed,
>> the mighty restorer
>> of the temporal Throne of David?

Or would Jesus,
> as Joseph held,
>> establish a spiritual Kingdom of Heaven on earth?

>>> But the only answer to these conjectures
>>> was the breathing of the sea
>>> and the whisper of the wind.

❦

"Can any good come out of Nazareth?"
>said the candidate Nathaniel.

>For here intersect the caravans
>of gentiles and heathens
>and here the mountains are wild
>and the men grow strong and fierce.

>Here Jesus grew up.

Nothing extraordinary happened.

>Jesus helped his mother.
>He smelled the fresh tabor oak and cedar
>as his father hewed and chiseled it.
>>His eyes kindled with love
>>as he watched his baby brother James.
>>>He listened with strange intensity
>>>as the oddly costumed caravan travelers
>>>exchanged stories of marvelous places
>>>beyond the mountains and across the seas.

AT THE appropriate time
    as with an ordinary mortal
        a fragment of the Father
            indwelt the five-year-old mind of Jesus.
And now in concert with the midway creatures and seraphim
    this marvelous Thought Adjuster
    assumed the responsibility
    for the Creator Son incarnate.

❧◎❧

THE accident was the fault of no one.

The aggressive and adventurous youth
was trapped on the roof by an unseasonable sandstorm.
    Blinded, Jesus struggled to the steps
        and tumbled down them.

        The heart of the universe skipped a beat
        but Jesus was unharmed.
            Even so, for months after,
            a frightened Mary kept him by her side.

❧◎❧

IT WAS the season of security,
    parents knew all things.
        And questions, questions, questions
            came in torrents from this
                inquisitive, searching child.
One day the earth
    trembled and moved
        forebodingly underfoot.
"Father, why did this happen?"
"I do not know my son."
His father did not know!
    Puzzled, Jesus turned away.

VISITORS!
    Zacharias and Elizabeth came from Judah
    and they brought young John!
Jesus and John
    enriched each other with smiles
    as they played with blocks and sand atop the house.
They were unaware of the portentous subjects
being discussed in hushed tones by the grownups below.

JESUS learned.

He pleasured when after the rainy season
the garden of earth burst into
extravagant and fragrant life.
He marveled at the steam
    rattling his mother's pots
    and contemplated the white snow
    melting in his hands.
He climbed the hills hand in hand with Joseph,
    where the sea winds blew cool and clear,
    and beheld the breathtaking panorama of Galilee
    not knowing it was a fragment of his own creation!

When light had passed away
    in the magic of sunset
        Jesus would lie atop the house
        and study the flawless silver embroidery
        of the silent stars above.

And when his young mind could not cope
        he would humble himself in some quiet spot
            and have a little talk with his Father in heaven.

JESUS was an enigma to his parents.

>He was non-contending in a physical way
>>and it was the stalwart Jacob
>>the stonemason's son
>>who was the self-appointed champion of Jesus
>>>against bullies and abuse.

>And yet
>when moral issues were at stake
>>Jesus had bountiful courage.

Joseph recalled the day the elders came.

>They admonished and upbraided Joseph
>for the drawing Jesus had made of his teacher.

>"Such things are graven images!"
>>bellowed one of the angry men.
>Suddenly, silhouetted in the doorway
>>was the small figure of Jesus.

WITH incredible composure
>he marched into the circle of towering adults.

>He defended his actions with resolute self-control
>>and poise.

And then Jesus vowed he would never draw or model again.
>"I will in all such matters
>abide by the wishes of my Earth father,"
>Jesus said, his head held high.

The elders marveled, and they left without another word.

Alone

   in the stillness of the hills

     the human mind of Jesus
     had a growing awareness
          of prolific scope and implication.

     The single personality
     had not yet grasped its twofold nature
         yet even at twelve Jesus knew
            he was to perform a divine mission.

Passover!

In Jerusalem!

>"Oh Israel, hope in the Lord"
>chanted the women as the caravan
>>neared the brow of the Mount of Olives.

The blood sprang in Jesus' veins!
>He thought his heart would burst
>>as the sacred city came into view!

>There below
>>glistening in the afternoon sun
>>>was the sight Jesus had hungered for. . .

>>He never forgot the feeling of
>>the fresh April breeze in his ecstatic face
>>as his eyes devoured the
>>>spectacle of his Father's house,
>>>the sacred Temple of Jerusalem.

BUT THERE was no time to lose!

Already the pilgrims were winding their way down the slopes
    toward the magnificent city.
        Soon he would be in his Father's house!

The streets were filled with throngs
of men and women and children afoot
costumed in picturesque finery from all over the world.
It was a splendid panorama of Jewry.
    All seemed joy and peace and plenty
        and the heart of Jesus rejoiced.

LATER Jesus sat alone
his head in his hands.

    By now he had looked deeper
    and now he had seen the thorns
    of ignorance and hypocrisy.

So many unseemly pictures tortured his mind.

How the careworn faces stared vacantly ahead
    as they jostled by.

How the money changers and merchants and harlots
    fouled the sacred temple with their coarseness.

How in the name of his Father
    the protesting animals were slaughtered
    by bloodied-handed priests
        as though to appease some venal despot!

    Mary and Joseph were confused
        as Jesus withdrew in silence
            weighed down by the
                crush of many contradictions.

THE WEEK of Passover was long.
　　Blow after blow of disillusionment
　　　　struck the sensitive nature of Jesus.

On Passover Eve
　　　　the gates of gold opened
　　　　　　and glorious waves of enlightenment
　　　　　　flooded the mind of Jesus.

His heart was moved to immeasurable compassion
　　for the dark, deluded minds of humankind.

A messenger of intense light
　　appeared to him and said:

　　"The hour has come.
　　It is time to be about your Father's business."

WHEN the returning Pilgrims reached Jericho they realized their mistake.

Jesus was gone!

Mary assumed he would return with the men, Joseph, with the women.

A crescendo of dreadful anxiety
    mounted in their hearts
        as they began to retrace
            their steps back to Jerusalem.

BUT JESUS was not lost.

    Even at this moment his youthful voice
    was being heard in the marble halls of the temple.

    His profound questions
    perplexed and dumbfounded
        the richly robed priests and scholars.

Why could not the mothers of Israel
    worship in the temple with the men?
Why were frightened dumb animals slaughtered
    to appease a loving Father-God?
Why was the Father's house used
    as a den of commerce and vice?
Would the Messiah re-establish the earthly throne of David?
    Or would he inaugurate a spiritual
        kingdom of heaven on earth?

AS THE scholars shifted and weighed
 these ponderous questions
 one leaned forward and growled to another:
 "He's from Nazareth; we might have known."

Yet the beautiful young man
 offended few;
 he was so gracious
 the power of his innocence so appealing
 his humility so engaging.

On the fourth day
 he was invited into the inner circle!
 The great men moved and adjusted to make room for Jesus
 so he could express his personal views
 on prayer and worship.

It was there and then
 on the brink —
 with a tremendous success within his grasp —
 that Joseph and Mary found him at last.

"My son," cried Mary,
 "Why have you so treated your parents?
 For three days we have searched for you in great fear.
 What caused you to desert us?"

A LL EYES were on Jesus.
    A moment before he was
    poised to impart and reveal to men
    the wisdom and love of his Eternal Father. . .

N OW THE Creator of this Universe
    stood accused by his mother's words
    and his father's eyes.

With supreme calm and restraint
    Jesus broke the silence.
    "Why have you thus been seeking me?
    Did you not know I would be in my Father's house,
    about my Father's business?"

    All were astonished at these words,
    and withdrew from the family.

    "Come my parents.
    Each of us did what he believed best.
    Let us go home."

O N THE return trip,
    when they reached the brow of Mount Olivet
        Jesus did an amazing thing.
            As waves of emotion racked his body
            Jesus raised his staff
            and shouted at the distant city:

            "Oh Jerusalem, Jerusalem!
            Your people are but pitiful slaves to Rome
                and their own chains of tradition.

            I shall return to cleanse your temple!
            I will deliver my people!"

Joseph and Mary were awed by these words.

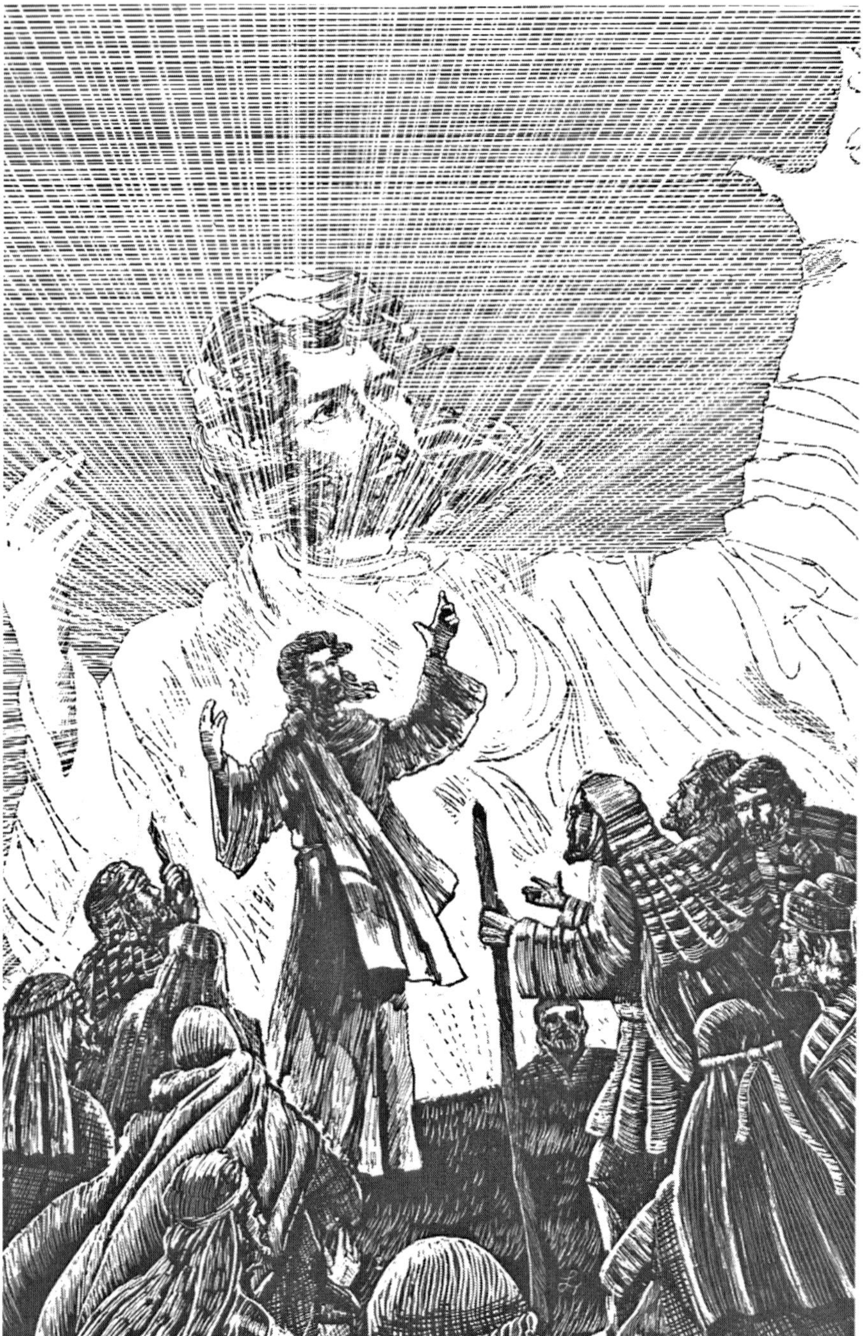

JESUS:
God and Man

III

"...the time has come..."

WHEN JESUS WAS ALMOST FIFTEEN
A TERRIBLE TRADGEDY STRUCK.

>Joseph was killed.

>The heavy burden of responsibility
>fell upon Jesus' shoulders.
>>Alone in the hills
>>he pondered his problems,
>>problems no other mortal mind
>>could share or understand.

LESS than a month later
the faithful of Nazareth assembled
to hear Jesus conduct his birthday synagogue service.
His voice was authoritative and manly
as he read from the scriptures.

"Fear not, for I am with you.
Be thou not afraid, for I am your God,
I will strengthen you, I will help you,
I will uphold you with the right hand
of my righteousness.
For I am the Lord, your God.
And I will hold your right hand saying,
Fear not, for I will help you!"

Those who were there that night
never forgot how commanding were those
broad shoulders and that wonderful face
in the glow of the candles.

Never had Jesus been so
powerful, compassionate, and noble.

YET THE people of Nazareth still debated about Jesus.

How could such a man of impressive physical prowess
> with so dynamic a stature
> so brilliant and optimistic
> > refuse to join the cause of the Zealots?

It must be more than family responsibility.

Even James did not understand
the strange silences of Jesus.
> To all his inquiries
> the reply never varied:
> "My hour has not yet come."

O H, HOW she loved him!

    How she loved that noble brow
    and the passionate tenderness of his eyes.

    The beautiful Rebecca looked imploringly
    at Jesus as her father talked to him.

But her heart sank as
    Jesus gently, resolutely, and firmly said no.
    He could not abandon his family.
        He could not marry Rebecca,
            or any woman.
        He was not free.
        He was a child of destiny.

The sweetness of the pain
    stayed in Rebecca's heart all her life
    as she followed her beloved Jesus.

Unseen
Rebecca watched from the shadows, for love asketh nothing —
    for love is sufficient unto love.

        And so it was until the end.

IT HAD been twenty-two years now
since the bestowal birth in Bethlehem.

    And now Jesus
        with serious dignity
        installed James as the head of the family.

        Though yet sending sums of money home,
        Jesus could now be freer
        to pursue his Father's business.

        Now began the most astounding,
        the most multi-faceted career
        ever to take place upon Urantia.

NEVER had such a man walked the earth.

    The sinewy smith of Sepphoris
    whose anvil rang with such authority
  yet whose eyes were incredibly gentle . . .

The impressive Galilean whose words
    so changed the life of Stephen that he would one day
        be a supreme martyr for Jesus the Christ . . .

The brilliant Nazarethian carpenter who refused
    to head an illustrious school in Damascus . . .

The creative boatbuilder of Capernaum
    whose original crafts skimmed the Sea of Galilee
      with speed and safety never known before . . .

The strange Jew, who when offered an important post
      in a new university in Alexandria replied:
        "My hour has not yet come."

The scribe of Damascus who traveled to Rome
  with Gonad and Ganid, father and son from distant India . . .

  So many candles these great men lit,
      candles that one day would become flaming torches
        for Jesus the Christ . . .

Yet few knew that the first flicker
    of their spiritual flame
        was ignited by the Son of God himself.

As a caravan master he taught
As a tent maker he taught
As a Jewish tutor he taught
    and always the message was the same:

    The mercy and love of God the Father
    The faith-sonship of each man
    The brotherhood of mankind.

Jesus taught the most when he said the least.
His language was universal.

    No man or woman or child was ever the same
    after they had been surprised
    by the benevolent kindness
    of those eyes.
        No heart was ever the same
        after it had been invaded
        by that sympathetic smile.

The presence of Jesus penetrated
    the most sullen frown or scowl
    and opened a path
    to the laughing, struggling, toiling,
        sweet-thinking soul of each human being.

Y ET JESUS, whose kingly bearing
  and gracious manner
  was so coveted by the Emperor of Rome
  and whose spell-binding logic
  held sway over the finest minds of Urmia,
  was the magnificent specimen of manhood
  who knelt down to soothe a lost child
  and patiently searched
    until he could restore him
      to his grateful mother.

S EE HIM! This too was Uncle Joshua
  whose face was so expressive and tender
  when he told the children stories
  and whose wonderful laugh
  rang so courageously and innocently.

T HE mission of Joshua the Teacher finally was over.

So many who were enriched by the spiritual fragrance
of this man would one day embrace the message
  of Jesus the Christ and become as
  beacons unto the earth . . .
Yet none knew they had met the Master face to face.

THERE remained a task of greatest importance.

    All of Nebadon was held spellbound
    as Jesus turned his steps northward
    toward the towering,
        eternally snow-peaked Mount Hermon.

Jesus took leave of his young companion Tiglath
and ascended into the heights of the mountain alone.

For five momentous weeks
Jesus held unbroken communion with his Eternal Father.

Jesus then asked
    to be permitted to face his fallen children
        as a man, a faith-son of God.

The prayers and hearts of the universe
were centered upon the drama of Urantia.
    But none could help
        no seraphim, no midwayer, no celestial being or power.

There was only Joshua ben Joseph
and his faithful Thought Adjuster.

NOW THE powers of Darkness descended ruthlessly
on a mere man, the lowest will creature of Nebadon.

They must destroy the resolve of Jesus —
They must break the circuit of his human faith!

The last residue of Universe sympathy vanished
for the children of darkness
as the deceivers sought to crush the will of Jesus.

BUT THEY had reckoned on the vulnerability of a man —
Not mortal man made invincible
by faith-submission to the will of the Eternal Father.

So on that summer afternoon
amid the stillness of nature
Joshua ben Joseph, the Son of Man
wrested dominion from his fallen children of sin.

"Let my Father's will be done.
May the Ancients of Days judge you with mercy."

THE rebellion,
    fostered in deceit and arrogance and narcissism
        was crushed with the irresistible power
            of humility, faith, mercy and justice.

As the unworthy children of Michael were silenced forever
    the faithful rejoiced as glory followed glory.

A SILENT and changed Jesus returned to the anxious Tiglath.

    In the weeks that followed
    Jesus spent many seasons
    in communion with his Father in Heaven.

    In time he donned his apron
    and resumed his boatshop labors with Zebedee,
        as he patiently waited his hour.

MEANWHILE John the Baptist
    was making his turbulent way
        up the valley of Jordan.

    "The kingdom of Heaven is at hand! Repent!"
was John's message,
    and Jesus worked on.

John reached Pella in January.

    On a Sunday
    just before the noon rest
        Jesus laid down his tools.

    "My hour has come," he said to his brothers.

    "Let us go to John."

SO IT was that on a fateful Monday in January
    John was astonished
    when he saw Jesus
    standing there before him,
    having patiently waited his turn.

In reply to the master's request for baptism,
    John said: "But it is I who need to be baptized by you."
    But Jesus was determined.
        He would set an example,
            John would baptize him.

JESUS stood before John
    a perfected mortal of Urantia.

    As John's trembling hands touched Jesus
    the Thought Adjuster of the Son of Man departed
    thus ending the mortal career of Joshua ben Joseph.

    Moments later the Divington-glorified spirit
    descended upon Jesus again, saying,

    "This is my beloved Son
    in whom I am well pleased."

THE face of Jesus transformed into radiant rapture
    as he beheld a vision of himself as Michael,
    the Creator Son of all of Nebadon.

THE Divine Son had found his Father,
    The Universal Father had found his Son,
    and they speak to one another.

THE countenance of Jesus
    showed the sublime repercussions of his triumph.

Now in silence he took leave of
    the wonder-struck mortals around him
        and made his way alone
            to the Perean hills to the east.

No human being
    saw the Son of God
        until forty days and nights had passed.

TWO minds had been made one.
>It was the season of momentous meditation
>>in the lofty, precipitous hills of Pella.

Monumental decisions were made and sealed.

Jesus would not pander
>the greed of human appetites
>>for bread and pomp and power.

Jesus was resolved as he returned
>with majestic strides to the
>>green shores of the Jordan.

He would exemplify
>the far-seeking ideal
>>of creature life for all of Nebadon
>>in accordance with the will
>>>of the Eternal Father.

His face shown triumph —
>His head was crowned with glory
>>greater than any earthly symbol.

JESUS lingered with the multitude
    of John's camp
        and began to select the men
            who would carry the torch.

    The Peerless Andrew —
        who would be called chief by the others,
        eldest and ablest of the twelve,
        a gifted judge of men.

Andrew's brother Simon Peter —
    vacillating, impetuous, mercuric
    the supreme orator.
    In the long term Jesus would
        temper his nature into steel and dedication.

Then were selected the Sons of Thunder
    James and John Zebedee.
    James, a dichotomous mixture of fire and ice —
    most feared by Herod Agrippa,
    first to fall after Jesus.
        John, the youngest apostle —
        who alone of the twelve would stand fearlessly
            at the foot of the cross
                and weep for the Master.

JESUS looked for the last time into
    the human face of John the Baptist
        and with the four fledgling apostles
            departed for Cana.

ON THE westward journey
    Jesus met Nathaniel and Philip
        and said simply: "Follow me."
            And they did.

Philip, called the curious —
    pragmatic and thorough, the supreme steward
        whose wife would one day follow him
            into martyrdom.

Nathaniel the honest —
    guileless and proud
        endowed with mirth, poetry and philosophy
        he won the hearts of all his brother apostles

            save one.

RUMORS were rampant:
    "The deliverer has come."
    "Jesus will assert his Messianic authority at
                the wedding feast."

The news spread quickly
    and many of Galilee traveled to Cana.
    Mary was joyful
    and attended the expected coronation
        with great anticipation.

All eyes were fixed on Jesus
    during the feast
        but nothing happened.
Late in the evening the wine supply ran dry.
Mary was seen going into the garden to appeal to Jesus.
She returned radiant with joy!
    What had Jesus told her?

Wait — see what they are drawing from
    the water jars? Wine!

A miracle! The six jars of water were now
    six jars of wine!
        A sign! The apostles were thrilled!

JESUS sat alone
    listening to the seaside waves
  his head in his hands.
        The stars paled and the sky lightened
        before the meditation was over.
The miracle was unintended.
        He must not ignite the human appetite
        for easy solutions, for bread and wonders.

            He must be more careful.

"**AT LAST!**"
>thought Simon Peter
>as he walked with swift steps along the road,
>his paraphernalia on his broad back.

At last, a task!
>The summer months of training were over.
>So impatient was Simon Peter
>so anxious to do something!

Men, women and children—
>The Master had said to meet with them,
>to talk with them,
>to teach them and learn from them. . .

>>and to select one of them as an apostle candidate.

>In two weeks Peter and the rest
>>would be back with Jesus.
>>For now, he welcomed the new challenge.

>>Peter smiled to himself as he plunged on.

THE CELESTIAL beings of Nebadon
looked down upon an amazing sight.

Twelve men kneeling in a circle of living faith
around the Creator Son of the Universe. . .
Simple, basic men of Urantia
    who would overcome the world.

In the circle was Matthew —
    a resourceful and clever tax collector
    who would secretly supplement the cause
    and exhaust his own funds.

Thomas Didymus —
    a carpenter and stone mason
    with a keenly analytical mind
    a chronic doubter balanced with courageous loyalty.

Side by side knelt the twins,
    James and Judas Alpheus —
    simple and common fishermen
    an inspiration to all of limited vision,
        true and faithful spirit Sons of God.

SIMON the Zealot —
> fierce firebrand of agitation
> whose unquenchable enthusiasm could inspire
>> the weakest and most feeble heart.

>> Judas Iscariot —
>> the enigmatic Judean
>> the collector of grievances
>> the faith-adventure of Jesus.

Beginning with Judas Iscariot
> Jesus laid his hands on each man
>> and anointed them with prayer.

JESUS now spoke of a spiritual kingdom,
of the brotherhood of mankind.
He spoke of a new way of life :
> A way of superb self-respect
> A way of poise and balance
> A way of compassionate action.

The apostles were to live in light and life
as though citizens of an already-realized
Kingdom of God.

On that Sunday morning
> in the emerald highlands of Capernaum
> Jesus entrusted the divine brotherhood of man
>> to the direction of human minds.

THE glorious day was here!

>The long journey to Jerusalem
>would be spent teaching and ministering
>to the people of the Jordan.

>A fond embrace from the families,
>a kiss of goodwill and love,
>and the twelve were ready to leave.

But where was the Master?

Andrew found him at last, on the beach.
>A lonely, solitary figure in a boat,
>his tanned cheeks were wet with tears.

"What is it, Master? On this day of days you weep?"
>"Andrew,
>I am saddened because
>>none of my father Joseph's family
>>have come to wish us Godspeed."

Then he drew his body up
>and he was himself again.

>>The great adventure had begun.

THE sojourn down the beautiful valley
    was leisurely and peaceful,
        the message well received.
By the time the gallant band passed the towering gates
    of Jerusalem the city was brimming
        with spring, and festive Passover throngs.
The Passover pilgrims heard a new message . . .
    like fresh air it came, clear and sweet
        and it seized the imaginations of many.
Even the priest Nicodemus, hidden by shadows,
    listened to the sonorous voice
        and marveled at the words.
Later in the home of the Greek Flavious
    surrounded by forbidden works of art
        Nicodemus looked into the face of Jesus
            and was enraptured by his wisdom and grace.
Nicodemus became fascinated by this religion
    that prescribed being born again
        and proscribed only pride and fear.

THE elite of Jerusalem sighed with relief
    when the upstart group
        and their compelling self-assured young leader
            left the holy city and journeyed northward.

F OR more than a year
        Simon the Zealot had lived with Jesus
            but he still had cause to shake his head and mumble.
Why were they here among the hated Samaritans?
These Godless gentiles were a waste of time.

Now Simon looked up in astonishment.
        There, at the Well of Jacob was Jesus,
            and he was talking to a Samaritan . . . woman!
A disturbed murmur ran through the ranks of the apostles.

        "Go thy way," the Master was saying,
        "This day begins a new life.
            You shall be a daughter of the Most High."
She left, and proclaimed to all of Sychar
        that she had met the deliverer!

A S THE summer shadows lengthened
        crowds flocked to Jacob's Well
            to hear Jesus.
The apostles marveled at his magic
        how the glorious affection in his eyes
        and the warmth of his message
        won the hearts of the Samaritans
            and quenched their spiritual thirst.

THE news came:
>John the Baptist was dead,
>murdered by Herod Antipas.

>For more than a year and a half
>John had languished in a filthy cell
>>sustained only by a single lifting message
>>>from Jesus.

>>Yet John was faithful to his charge
>>and to his beloved Jesus
>>to the end.

"THE time has come,"
>the Master said,
>>"To proclaim the kingdom openly,
>>and with power."

>>>✦

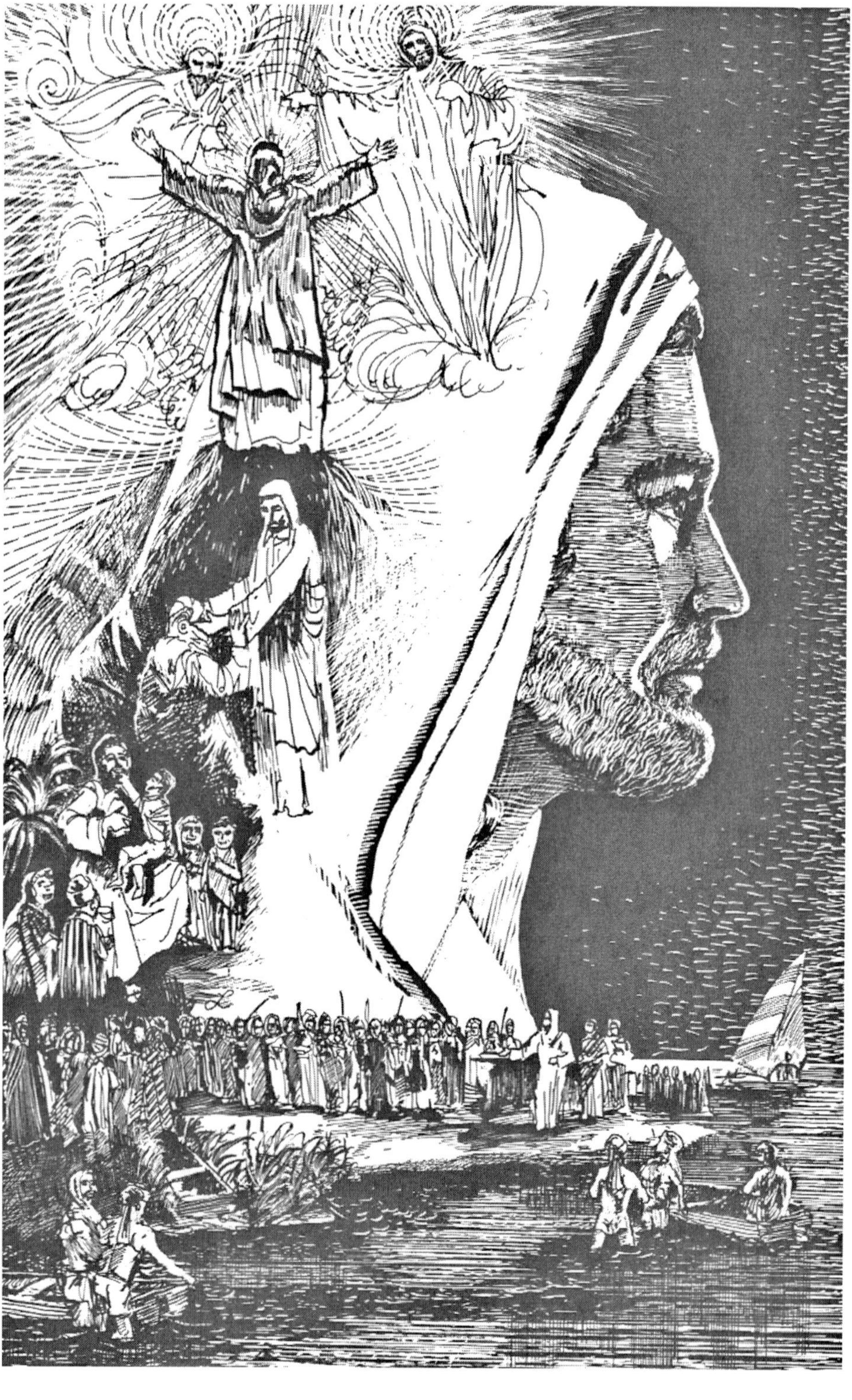

JESUS:
God and Man

IV
"...who do men say I am?.."

THE SIGHT OF CAPERNAUM WAS WELCOME,
lush and green with the season of the rains.

How the words of Sister Ruth
soothed the human heart of Jesus
as they sat in the tiny boat,
white in the Galilean moonlight.

THE sun dropped out of sight —
The apostles could hear the multitudes coming
> long before they arrived.
>> Wagging tongues had fanned the flames of hope
>>> and a motley army of nearly seven hundred
>>> afflicted humans
>>>> marched on the home of Zebedee.

"I saw him! He turned water into wine!"
"He drove unclean spirits from a young man!"
"Surely he is the deliverer! Surely
he will relieve our adversities!"
"Oh Master! Save us! Help us!"

The Master appeared on the porch
> and a supreme expectant stillness descended over all.

> The wonderful voice was accented with compassion,
> and a desperate appeal to the Father's judgment
> caused an incredible happening.

100

UPON the word of Jesus
    withered limbs were made whole,
unclean bodies were made radiantly pure,
sightless eyes wept as the gift of
    light pierced their dark prison,
long silent throats sang out joyous praises!

The apostles embraced each other ecstatically.
The news radiated from Capernaum like lightning.
The Wonder-Worker is come!
The Messiah is here!

But the next day when tumultuous crowds came
to praise Jesus, he was not there.

JESUS was alone in the hills.
>His perplexed human mind
>>had spent a sleepless night.

>Jesus knew.

>He had not healed or made whole a single
>>bitter and withered heart. . .
>He had not cleansed a single mind polluted
>>with selfishness . . .
>He had not given spiritual light
>>to the morally sightless. . .
>The kingdom had not been advanced
>>by this wonder-working.

>He sent word to the apostles:

>It is time to quit this place —
>this scene of the wondrous happenings.

>Much work needed to be done.

AS THE proclaimers of the Gospel
 tarried and taught in the cities of Galilee
 their eyes and ears were extended
 to all parts of Israel.
The fisherman,
David Zebedee had created a vast living net
 of observers and messengers
 that blanketed hill and valley
 and captured an abundant
 harvest of happenings,
 reporting them with
 dramatic swiftness
 to the fishers of men.

HEROD Antipas listened intently
>to the news about the strange carpenter.

>The Capernaum miracle had aroused his sleeping fears.

>>Could this Jesus of Nazareth
>>>be the revengeful resurrection
>>>>of John the Baptist?

These wonders,
>>what did they mean?
>>The leper of Iron, had he really been made clean?
>>Had a dead boy been made to live again?
>>Was a woman cured by touching his robe?
>>A lunatic made rational?
>>The centurion, no doubt about his testimony —
>>>Jesus said the word and his servant was cured.

>And now he was back in Jerusalem
>for the Passover feast.
>Today at the pool of Bethesda
>>a cripple was made to walk.

FINALLY Herod spoke.
    "Watch him.
        I care not if he says he can
            forgive a woman's sins
        or if he pretends to cure the gullible. . .
        Nor do I care about his bewildering stories.

        Nonetheless— he may be up to something.
        He bears watching."

With a wave of his hand Herod dismissed his sinister servants.

WITH THE coming of another season of the sun
    a tent city sprang up
        on the Sea of Galilee, at Bethsaida.

From the distant parts of the empire they came,
    the sick in body and the impoverished in spirit. . .
    from beyond the Euphrates
    from the lands of strange languages
        came an unending, multi-colored river of humanity.

AMONG the responsive faces that jammed the Zebedee home
were now hard, cold countenances of suspicion
that watched and listened to Jesus
with relentless intensity.

All eyes looked up this day in astonishment!
There slowly, slowly from the roof
a bed was being lowered!
A pathetic paralytic was now at the
feet of Jesus, pleading to be cured.

"Son, thy sins are forgiven thee.
Rise, take up thy bed and walk."
The commanding assurance of those eyes
was irresistible.
The man rose, and all gave way as he walked
through the crowd!
All praised God,
such happenings had never been seen before.

Only three spies returned to Jerusalem,
the other three were won over to the kingdom.

"BETTER the Words of Law should be burned
than delivered to a woman . . ."
        so said the rabbinic teachings.
The Master hurled a fearless proclamation
        that pierced the mists of ignorance:
"In the kingdom all are equal
there is neither male nor female —
all are spiritual sons and daughters of the living God."

Suzanna,   Martha,   Milcha,
  Joanna,   Rachel,   Ruth,
    Elizabeth,   Nasanta,   Celta,
        and Agaman were later joined by
        Rebecca of Arimathea
        and Mary Magdalene.
        As deaconesses of the Master
        they uplifted their downtrodden sisters
        and carried the word with great power.

IN THE black days yet to come
        all twelve would stand courageously
        their ranks unbroken, their spirits undaunted,
        at the foot of the cross.

Only the apostle John would stand with them.

IN THE afterglow of the March sunset
    Jesus stood on a hill overlooking Nazareth.
    In his carefree days of youth
    he climbed this hill with happy steps
    hand in hand with Father Joseph.

    The human heart of Jesus swelled
    as he made his way down to the city.
        He knew each fig and olive tree,
        each cactus hedge and home.

A lonely trumpet blast
heralded the sunset and echoed in the darkening hills.

A MAGNIFICENT Nazareth morning
found the synagogue jammed.
Jesus ascended the platform
healthy, strong, and tanned
confident and steady,
but not otherwise different.
Was this not Jesus, the carpenter?

Jesus gazed into cynical, doubting faces.
Slowly he unrolled the scroll and started to read.
His discourse was gracious and wise.

But, after speaking, brutal faces
forced their way close to him.

OMINOUS clouds of anger were forming.
    Bitter, angry words were hurled at him.
"We know you — you are no prophet!"
"Do a wonder — are we not good enough for a miracle?'
"Where is your family?"

       The storm broke.
       The pent up anger of the town
           that Jesus dared to outgrow
              now vented itself in violence.
       Rough handed men seized Jesus
           and rushed him from the synagogue
           to the brow of a lofty cliff.

       In a moment they would surely hurl him
       to his death!

BUT they did not.

      Jesus suddenly turned, faced them,
         and slowly folded his arms.
      They shrank back as he made his way
         through their ranks.

      Before they could reform their purpose he was gone.
      His heart was laden with sorrow
         as he made his way back to camp.

THE near-disaster at Nazareth a month before
had sobered the apostles.

But this day was different!

In the warm sunshine of Galilee
nearly five thousand faces turned eagerly toward Jesus.

The two dried fishes and five barley loaves
were distributed, and the multitude ate their fill!

This is what they had been waiting for!

Moses fed their fathers manna in the wilderness,
and now the Son of David had come to supply their needs.

The joyous chorus crescendoed,
      this was the day of deliverance!
        The mob thundered as one voice, "Make him King!"

SUDDENLY Jesus stood upon a rock
    majestic and immobile.
His hand raised, the crowd silenced.

"No, my children," he said.
In the rosey glow of that marvelous twilight
He turned back their enthusiasm—
    He stunned their leaders—
    He crushed their hopes.
        "If you must have a king,
        he concluded, "let God the Father
        reign in your hearts."

The disciples were stung by the rejection.
    The people deserted in droves.

"ONLY two months," thought Peter,
"and how the tide has turned!"

He watched the thin ranks of the remaining faithful
    assemble for the Master's farewell.
Only two months before
    with a single word from Jesus
        five thousand would have borne him through the gates
    of the holy city and crowned him king.
Since then there had been few ears for the gospel.
    Even at Passover the crowds
    were frigid and indifferent.
Then Jesus gave that scathing sermon at Capernaum!
    He aggressively denounced and scorned
    the hyprocrisy of the Sanhedrin,
    effectively embarrassing and enraging
        the powerful inner circle of Jerusalem.
Now all the synagogues were closed to the Master.

FINALLY, at this very moment,
    the blood-thirsty Sanhedrin officials
    were on their way to arrest Jesus.

The magic days seemed over.

Y ET WHEN Peter shouldered his way into the house
>he found Jesus confident and buoyant
>>his discourse lavish with hope, faith and courage.

Word came.
>Peter whispered the message to Jesus:
>His mother and his family were outside.

A look of pain flashed across that wonderful face.
>How a warm embrace from his mother
>or a gracious handshake from his brothers
>>would have helped a few weeks ago!
>But he must first finish his important discourse.

Jesus spoke with great power.
"I have no mother. I have no brothers.
Behold my mother and my brothers!
For whosoever does the will of his Father in heaven,
 they are my brother and my sister and my mother!"

Jesus would talk to his family,
but it was too late!

The Sanhedrin was closing in!

BEFORE the boats were launched
       Jesus again sent regrets to his family
           and then the laden crafts made their way slowly
               across the smooth waters,
                   away from the malicious pursuers.
The crowds along the shore shrank away
       the oars creeked and dipped
              Jesus was on his way to the
              Phoenician coast.

THE season of the sun in Phoenicia was pleasant.
　　The gentiles responded
　　　　　　to the message of the kingdom.

This noontide,
　　under rustling mulberry trees
　　the apostles recounted the pleasant summer interlude
　　as they prepared for lunch.

Suddenly Jesus asked, "Who do men say I am?"

　　　　　　　　　　"Elijah."
　　　　　　　　　　"John the Baptist."
　　　　　　　　　　"Jeremiah, Master."
　　　　　　　　　　"Moses."
　　　　　　　　　　"Isaiah."

JESUS stood up,
　　and poised there at full height;
　　he swept his hand majestically at the apostles and said,

　　"But who do you say I am?"

ALL eyes were fastened on Jesus.
>Peter leaped to his feet.
"You are the deliverer, the
Son of the Living God."

THE words of Jesus were now heavy with import:

>"My Father has revealed this to your hearts.
You are my ministers, and upon this spiritual rock
I shall build a living temple of Spiritual Brotherhood.
To you I give the keys of the Kingdom."

THUS THE full revelation unfolded . . .
>Jesus: God and Man.

"Tell no man I am the Son of God."

THE night was silent, black as pitch.

       Andrew crept toward Jesus.

       "Master, the others sleep.
       I must unburden to you my anxiety
       about one of our brethren,
               Judas Iscariot."

"I understand. You do right to come to me, Andrew.
There is nothing we can do
save to continue to place
utmost faith in this apostle.

Rest now."

P ETER'S eyes grew heavy.
>It had been a long day.
>They began the ascent of Mount Hermon
>early that morning.

>>The splendid day had flown.
>>James and John were sleeping
>>Peter drifted off . . .

As a single man, they all awoke.

>>There was Jesus,
>>a vision of radiant splendor
>>speaking in a strange tongue to two celestial beings!

>>Gabriel and Melchizedek disclosed the success
>>>of the bestowal, the Eternal Son and Spirit
>>>>were satisfied.

Now A silver cloud approached.
    A voice said: "This is my beloved Son.
        Take heed of him."

The three apostles prostrated themselves in fearful worship.

    "Arise and fear not" said the Master.
    "You shall see even greater things than this."

    "But tell no man what you have seen
    until the Son of Man is risen from the dead."

Badly shaken and awestruck
    Peter, James and John descended the mountain.

SOMETHING was amiss.

    Philip and Matthew were red-faced and angry
        as they returned from the city.
Those ignorant gentiles had refused lodging
    for the Master!
They had been chased away from the city!
The Son of God had been scorned!

"Call down fire on them!"
    They all agreed.
        "Call down fire on them Master!"

The fine features of Jesus tightened.
    His eyes showed the strain of the past weeks
    and foreshadowed omens of more bitter days to come.

Would they never understand?
        "You know not what you say.
        Revenge is the mask of cowardice."
Jesus picked up his garments
    and started down the road.

The apostles followed
        each vaguely aware
            that he had somehow failed Jesus.

"**L**OOK!"
"It's him! In Jerusalem again!"
"That upstart carpenter is back!"
"How dare he teach in the temple?"

"The Romans have given him protection.
That's the only possible explanation."

"Nonsense, his disciples are frightened to death."

"Look! There is Eber. He is going to arrest Jesus!"
"Jesus is telling him not to fear,
to come closer."
"What's he telling Eber now?"

"They are leaving! They did not arrest him!"

"Eber! What is it? What did Jesus say?"

"Never a man so spoke," said Eber.

Eber went on his way with his befuddled assistants,
and reported the failure to the chief of the Sanhedrin.

He was incandescent with rage.

THEY CAME from everywhere,
    and they gathered at Magadan.
  Abner and the fifty from Bethlehem,
    the evangelistic corps, the women's corps,
    the messenger corps of David Zebedee.
Seventy were selected to go and teach the gospel.

Under a rain-washed sky the Master ordained and blessed them.
They went forth two by two.

⁓⦿⦿⦿⁓

THE Jordan was swollen with winter rains
    by the time the three men
      reached the ford at Bethany.
      Nathaniel and Thomas pleaded with Jesus.
      "Master,
      We were fortunate to get out of
      Jerusalem last time with our skins.
      It is too risky for you,
      too many plot your destruction."

  Jesus smiled and continued on.
      "I would give those teachers of Israel
      another chance to see the light
      at the feast of dedication."

⁓⦿⦿⦿⁓

"IS THIS your son?" asked the chief of the Sanhedrin.
"Was he indeed born sightless?
How is it that he now sees?"
The father spoke: "This is our son.
He was born blind. We do not know how it is
that he can see. Ask him, he is of age."
Josiah stepped forward.
"All I know is that I was born blind
and now I see. I believe this man is a prophet."
A volley of angry questions and accusations
burst from the lips of the priests.
"I have told you exactly, you did not believe.
Would you hear it again?
Do you wish to become his disciples?"

THE leaders rushed at Josiah, shouting abuse.
Undaunted, the courageous man
stood on a chair, and spoke for all to hear.
"Hear me. This man opened my eyes.
Only a man of God could do such things.
Never since time began have such things happened.
This man is from God."

JOSIAH was cast out of the synagogue.
Later that day he worshiped at the feet of Jesus.
Thus he joined the noble spiritual elite
of that day and that generation.

THE season of miracles seemed to pass.
Yet the message continued to take root
in the hearts of people.

Jesus left Jerusalem and turned eastward
traveling over the Jordan to the land of Perea.

Here the parables of the master
befuddled his enemies and
enlightened the faithful.

Within the folds of each story
was enchanting treasure
and matchless wisdom.

More and more the disciples understood the words:

"Behold I stand at the door and knock,
If any man will open I will come in."

THE MASTER was too late.

    Lazarus was   dead.
    The stone had sealed his tomb
        four days now.

"Where have you laid him?" asked Jesus.
    As he followed Mary and Martha
    His heart overflowed, and he wept.
"See, he weeps.
    How he loved Lazarus.
    Why did he not come sooner?"
Unseen, a mighty array of celestial beings were assembling.

"Take the stone away."
    The earth creatures watched in breathless silence.
    Jesus prayed.
        Then his voice boomed out:
        "Lazarus, come forth!"

Lazarus began to move! He sat up on the stone shelf.

"Loose him from his grave clothes and let him go."

ONLY THE two sisters and the apostles remained;
all the mourners had fled in terror.

Lazarus was confused.
    Had he really been dead?
    "Yes, my son," Jesus reassured.
        "What has happened to you will be the experience of all believers . . .
            though they shall rise in more glorious form."

    "I am the resurrection and the light!"

BREATHING heavily,
    the priest Caiaphas rose to his feet.
    "It is better that Jesus die,
        rather than the community perish.
    We have expelled nineteen members
        from our body —
            men too weak to act.
    The fact is plain:
    Jesus must die."

"SUCH A waste," thought Judas.
Using costly ointment for the Master's feet!

"Andrew," said Judas,
" this is expensive ointment that could be sold and the money given to the poor."

Jesus looked up.
"Leave her alone, all of you.
This woman saved this ointment to use on my body at my death.
She anticipates the death of the Son of Man.
She shall not be denied this act of love."

THE eyes of Judas flamed over
with rage and embarrassment.
He turned away, and said nothing.

But he thought of the coming visit to Jerusalem.

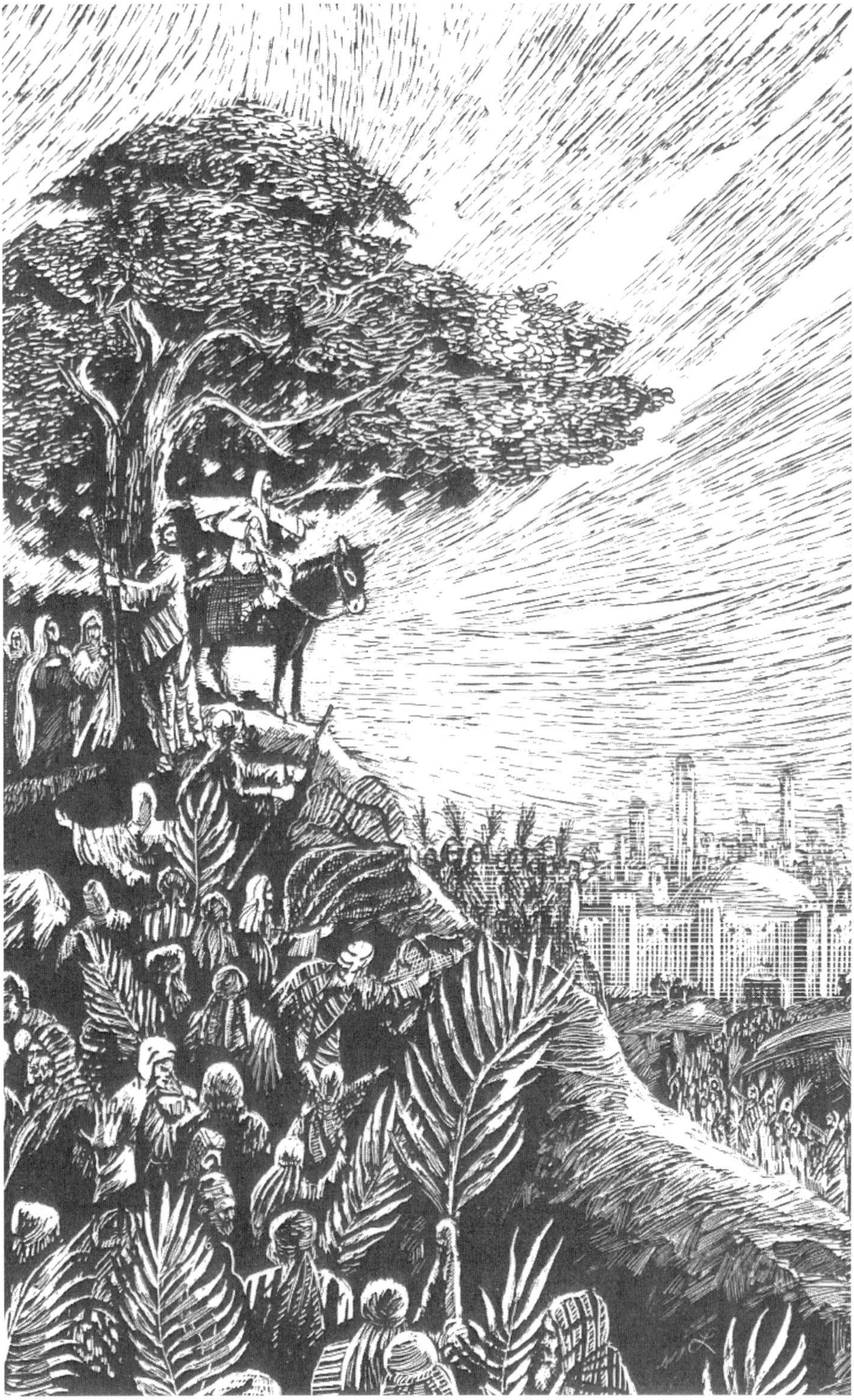

JESUS:
God and Man

V

"...you are about to reject the gift of God..."

"REJOICE GREATLY
    O daughter of Zion;
Shout, O daughter of Jerusalem.
    Behold,
    your king comes to you.
    He is just and he brings salvation.
    He comes as a lowly one, riding upon an ass. . ."

IT WAS like the old days!
    The multitudes came to him again
        and they sang "Hosanna in the highest!"
And they flung down their garments in his path
           . . . a welcoming carpet for the Son of David!

Jesus was his old self,
    light-hearted and ever-smiling
    until they reached the brow of Olivet
    and overlooked the mighty City of Zion.

The Multitude beheld that Jesus wept
    and as their songs dimmed away to silence,
    the voice of the Master
        rang out over the Valley of Kidron.

"Oh Jerusalem, you are about to reject the Son of Peace,
and turn your backs on the gospel of salvation . . .
    You are about to reject
        the gift of God!"

THE joyous tide
of praise and thanksgiving
began to rise again
as Jesus started down the mountain.

Then the gates of the city burst open
and throngs of people poured out
to greet the Master.

Jesus rode majestically
in the April sunshine
through a sea of waving palms
and smiling faces.

J UDAS was startled as a discordant voice
    rang in his ear:
        "Judas! Why so sad?
            My good friend!
                Cheer up and join us all
                as we proclaim your Jesus of Nazareth
                King of the Jews!
                    Ha! As he rides
                      through the gates of Jerusalem —
                          On an ass!"

        Judas shrank from the
        Laughing Pharisee.

B UT THE other apostles were enjoying
    The cheers and goodwill of the crowd.
        They expected the Master would make a speech
            to the multitudes from the temple steps.
        But after Jesus entered the city
        he suddenly dismounted
        and walked casually off.
            The crowds began to drift,
                and the golden moment slipped away,
                      unexploited.

THERE were no welcoming throngs
    the next morning, as Jesus led his apostles
        down the Mount of Olives
            and through the city gates.

The band was silent and apprehensive
    as they followed the Master
        into the cool shadows
            of the temple court
                where a small gathering of believers
                awaited them.

Already the daily din
    of the howling animals
        and shouting merchants had begun.

        Jesus mounted a teaching platform
                but he did not speak.

        His noble head was turned,
        apparently observing an argument.
        Suddenly the bellowing of a drove of bullocks
            added to the noise and confusion.

SILENTLY Jesus stepped down.
>Puzzled eyes were fastened on him
>as his confident, purposeful strides
>carried him across the court to the
>>distant animal stalls.
>>He paused only
>>>to snatch a whip
>>>>from the surprised hand of a cattle driver.

"Look! He is releasing the animals!"
>One by one Jesus was opening the stalls
>>and driving out the protesting beasts!
>>"No one dares stop him!"
>>>"He is driving the animals from the temple!"

The younger pilgrims were made bold
>by the seemingly invincible Jesus!
>>They overturned the table of a money changer!
>>And now another! And another!

The air was filled with the cries of the animals,
>the merchants and the money changers!
>>The powerful arm of Jesus rose and fell
>>>driving the baying and bleating menagerie
>>>>out on the street,
>>>>>at the heels of the
>>>>>>human parasites.

THEN suddenly, all was silent.

The temple had been cleansed.
   Once more the stalwart Galilean
    mounted a teacher's platform
     and his voice rang out:
"This day you have witnessed
that which has been written:
'My house shall be called a house of prayer,
But you have made it a den of thieves'!"

But he could not say more.
   A thunderous ovation of "hosannas"
    drowned out his words.

The apostles, impotent in their astonishment,
   watched the events as spectators.

     What would happen now?

IN FESTERING fury
   The Sanhedrin recounted
      the humiliations of the past two days:

         The brazen, tasteless way Jesus entered Jerusalem;
            How the ignorant masses praised him!
         The shocking and illegal clearing of the temple;
         How one by one their most brilliant intellects
                  were humbled like children when they
                        matched wits with Jesus.

But it was the hated Nazarene's
   last temple discourse that was the ultimate embarrassment.

The proud elite,
   the Pharisees and Scribes,
   the Sadducees and Herodians,
   stood by, timidly mute,
      as the matchless young orator
      attacked them with devastating effectiveness.

JESUS had spoken at first
    in tones of reconciliation
        but soon launched what seemed
            a scalding denunciation of all they stood for.

      "He called us hypocrites!"
      "False teachers!"

      "He said we unmercifully exploit the poor!"

      "He claimed that we pretend to be clean outside,
      but are defiled and corrupted within!"

      "He dares say these things, and more!"

"And then he has the incredible audacity
    to offer *us* mercy!"

      Caiaphas' bloodless lips curled
        in a smile of triumph.
            For the first time the vote was unanimous.

        Jesus must die!

THE Wednesday rest day
    came none too soon for the weary apostles.

    Jesus also showed the strain
    of the past two days
        as he prepared to go into the hills
            to visit with his Father.

    All stood apart.
        The Master was resolved that none
            would accompany him.
        Then the young lad, John Mark,
            approached Jesus
                offering him a basket of food and water.

Jesus smiled as he took the handle
    but John kept hold
        as he pleaded to follow Jesus into the hills.
        There they stood
            the Creator of the Universe
            and the young boy
                who wanted with all his heart
                    to be with him.

JESUS relented;
> John Mark followed him into the hills.

So it was that Jesus spent his last free day on Urantia
feeding the soul of a truth-hungry child,
and John enjoyed a splendid communion,
> sitting in the wind-swept grass
> and listening to the beloved words of Jesus.

THE CAMP envied John

    that he did dare to knock,
    and thus commanded the ministry
    of God and man,

        even on the brink
        of the terrible test to come.

Few in the camp noted the absence of Judas Iscariot.

EACH step Judas took
> left him more convinced than ever.
>> The wine of his traitorous escape from responsibility
>>> intoxicated his narcissistic soul
>>>> with dreams of grandeur and glory.

Caiaphas was impressed by him,
> he was sure of that.
>> The mighty priest certainly had
>>> splendid plans for Judas. . .

>>>> After this grim business was finished.

As Judas approached the camp of the Master
> his throat became dry,
>> his hands began to tremble.

>>> If only it was tomorrow night
>>>> and it was over!
>>>> It will be so much easier when it is over!

∽⊙ю☉∼

ANDREW watched the Master carefully.

    On this Thursday morning
    Jesus had led the entire camp
        of apostles and disciples
            to a secluded bower.

        Glorified in the golden sunlight
        the Master poured out his heart
           to his brethren.
Andrew pondered the magnificent man before him.

    Was it his imagination
        or were the Master's words
        richer, more profound, more urgent than ever?
        Were those marvelous eyes
           glistening with even more love than usual?
        Was there a shadow of sadness,
           now and then, in that wonderful smile?

DAVID Zebedee also watched this day.

>His heart was like lead.
>He must speak to Jesus.

After lunch
>he caught the Master for a moment alone.
>David told the terrible news
>>about Judas Iscariot.
>>The Master's eyes bore down on David
>>>with a power only tenderness can wield.
>>>"We must trust the Father's will," he said.
>>At that moment word came from Abner.
>>He, too, saw the gathering of storm clouds.
>>David would cherish the message Jesus sent Abner:

"GO ON with your work.
>>If I depart from you in the flesh
>>it is that I may return to you in the spirit."

>The promise that followed
>would cheer and freshen many seeking,
>>weary hearts:

>"I will not forsake you.
>I will be with you to the end."

NATHANIEL had never seen
    the Master so calm,
        so composed,
            so supremely in command.

THE face of Jesus
    was softly gilded
        in the glow of the
            Passover candles.

His eyes seemed to peer into the distant ages.

AT LAST Jesus spoke again.
    "If the master was willing to wash your feet,
    why is it you are unwilling to wash
            one another's feet?"

It began to dawn on Nathaniel how tragically
    they had all failed Jesus again . . .
        on this night of all nights.
    The selfish arguments about seating,
    how their egoistic appetites had offended the Master!
    And how majestically and graciously
        Jesus had transcended them
            as he bent down to wash their feet!
                And now – where was Judas going?
            Off on some errand, no doubt.

Now that the Master had begun to teach again
    his magnificent words were the only sound in the room.
    "Love one another
        as I have loved you . . .
    Though I leave you
        I will be close to you . . ."

"BUT Master, where are you going? We will follow you!"

THE questions finally abated,
    and with a poignant gentleness
        the Master spoke of happier times
            under the blue skies of Galilee.
            The face of Jesus softened
            as he reminisced the days of gold.

            So many times the twelve
            had broken bread together!
            He recalled the joy of the wedding at Cana . .
            The day of the feeding of five thousand . . .

NOW Nathaniel knew: He really is leaving us!
>His heart could scarcely bear the weight
>>of these too-tender, too-touching moments.

As Jesus spoke to each of them in turn
>it was not the words
>>that made their souls burn,
>>>it was the unbearable sweetness and power
>>>in the Master's eyes as he gazed at them
>>>>as though from some imponderable
>>>>vista of anguish.

At the end of the evening
>they all sang together,
>these rugged and courageous comrades,
>>their eyes brimming in the flickering candlelight.

CELESTIAL beings and silent stars looked down
on the slopes of the Mount of Olives,

>>as later that night
the eleven men knelt in a circle.

In the mellow moonlight
Joshua ben Joseph
prayed with them one last time.

"The world knows little of you Father,
but I know you,
and I have revealed you to these men.

I promise them now,
that you shall always be with them,
as you have always been with me."

HOW heavy-laden Jesus seemed
    on this strange night!

John Mark watched Jesus as he drew away
    into the garden with Peter, James and John.

John Mark followed
and his eyes beheld the unfolding
    of an amazing drama.

Three times the Master prostrated himself in prayer
    while the nearby apostles dozed.
Three times the Master sought strength
    for his coming ordeal. . .
And three times he returned
    to find the weary trio asleep.

John Mark observed as Jesus spent his
    most desperate hour of human need
        without a word of solace.
Jesus seemed to tremble with emotion
when he asked if this terrible cup
might pass from his lips.

THEN THE courage of the Son of Man rose, as always.

He thought back to the days of Galilee —

The shimmering waters, silver and blue and beautiful.
He recalled his mother's smiles as he helped her in the home —
The warm hand of father Joseph as they ascended
        the hills above Nazareth.
How he had loved the music of the laughter
        of his younger brothers and sisters!

JOHN Mark saw that powerful back straighten,
    that noble head regain its majestic poise,
        and he heard the words that
            sounded like a call to battle:

"Oh Father,
if it be not your will
that this cup pass from me,
then Father your will,
not mine, be done!"

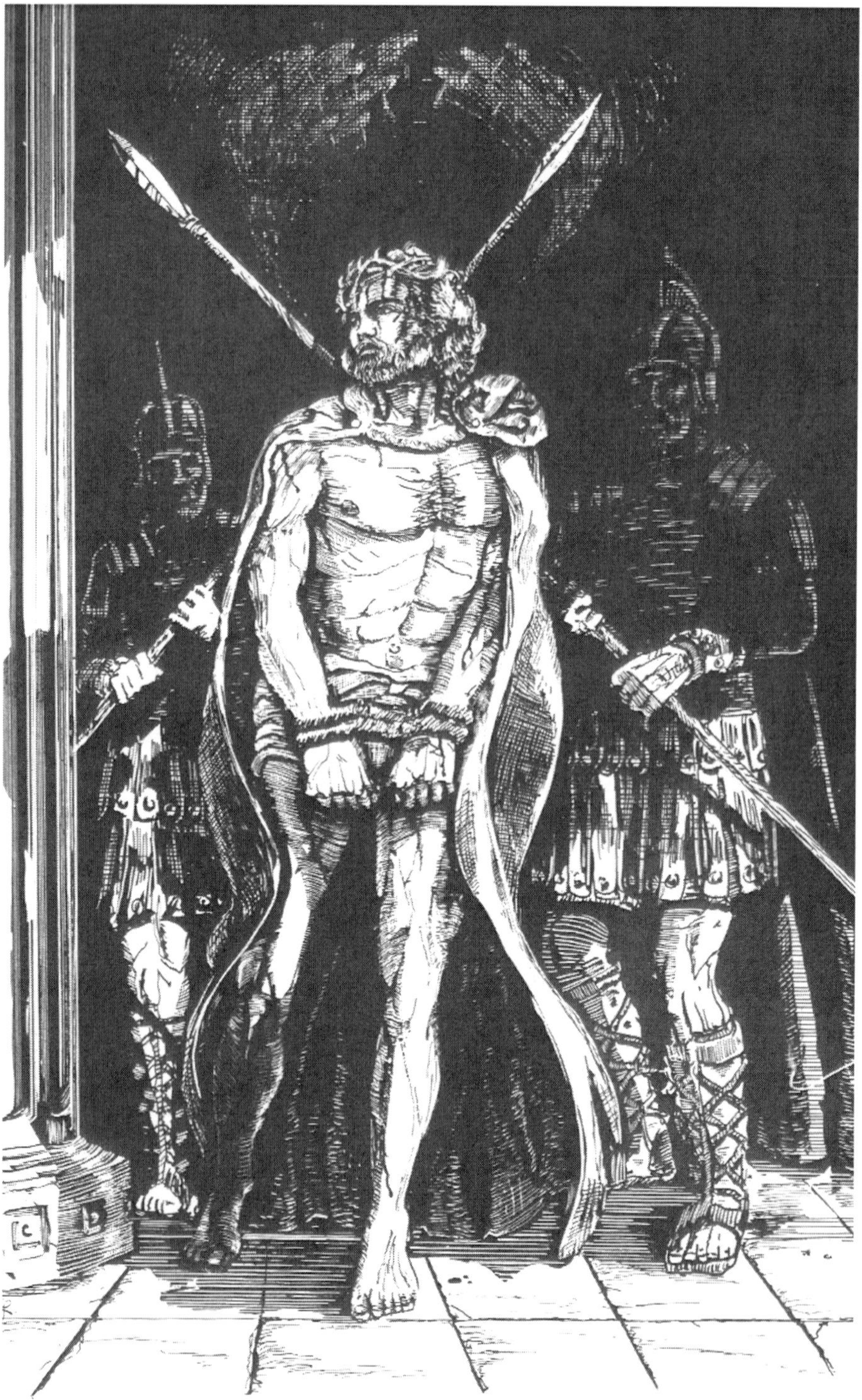

JESUS:
God and Man

VI

"...behold God and Man..."

IT WAS VERY LATE.

        Jesus stood alone in the moonlight
        watching the distant torches coming ever nearer,
        as the universe gazed down
        on the drama of Gethsemane.

J UDAS came into view,
    then the soldiers at his heels,
    their spears and armor
    gleaming in the torchlight . . .

The Master spoke first.
    "Whom do you seek?"
    "Jesus of Nazareth," said the captain.
    "I am he," said the supremely poised God of Creation.
But Judas would not be thwarted!
    He drew close and hailed the Master,
    kissing him on the forehead.

    Jesus said: "Friend. Is it not enough that you do this?
        Would you betray me with a kiss?"

AGAIN Jesus offered himself to the Romans
and this time they seized him and bound him.

> A single command stayed the eager and vengeful
> > swords of the apostles,
> > > and they began to flee
> > > > before the pursuing soldiers.

As Jesus started the fateful journey
> the courageous footsteps of John Zebedee
> > caught up with him,
> > > and continued in faithful cadence at the Master's side.

THE procession marched through the chilly night
to the house of the mighty Annas:
The silent Jesus;
the faithful John;
> the soldiers and the Jews.

> A single confused figure
> followed at the very end—
> > Judas Iscariot.

AS HE waited
Annas paced impatiently.

>Perhaps Jesus would agree to leave the country.
>>That would solve everything!
>But when the doors opened
>and the Master stood before him,
>>>even more commanding and majestic
>>>than Annas recalled him,
>>>>Annas knew it was hopeless.
>>It would be pointless to ask such a man to flee.

So Annas hurled his questions loudly
>>to conceal his own discomfort.
>>>>>>Jesus was silent.

But when Annas boasted of his power to save Jesus
>the Master admonished him.
>>In a flash an obsequious steward
>>>struck the face of Jesus.

The perplexed Annas ordered that Jesus be taken to Caiaphas.

"ARE you not one of his disciples?" asked the girl.
    Peter looked up from the glowing warmth of the fire.
        "I am not."
Another asked: "But did I not see you in the garden
    when they arrested him?
        Do you not follow him?"
                      "I do not know this man."
A third insisted: "But I have seen you in the temple with him!"
        "I am not his follower!
        I do not know him!
        I never heard of him!"
Moments later the crowing of the rooster
    broke the early morning air.
        Peter realized with crushing suddenness that,
        as the Master had warned,
        he had indeed denied Jesus.

Suddenly the massive doors creaked open,
    and as the procession passed
        Jesus looked on Peter with compelling pity
            and overwhelming love.

That look would live in the heart of Peter
    for the rest of his days.

THE Sanhedrin —
    Thirty arrogant and prejudiced judges
        and their false witnesses
            passed judgment on the Son of Man.
As they spewed out their passionate lies
    and unscrupulous exaggerations
   the Master met them
       with wondrous composure and eloquent silence.

Angered by his silent rebuke
    they smote him and spit in his face.
      Then they isolated him in a room
          where he was scorned and abused unmercifully.

A shudder of horror ran through Nebadon!

    Yet now Michael's greatest moments,
    his finest victories were being won.
       For all the universe Michael was triumphing over
         man's most terrible illusions: loneliness and separation.
The second meeting of the court
    decreed his guilt and ordered his death.
       The prisoner was not in the chamber.

       They dared not look into that innocent face again.

"TRUTH?"
    What is truth?" sneered Pilate
        turning away from his disturbing prisoner.

      The strange man before him was weary
        from the long sleepless night
          yet he held himself so nobly
            and his eyes were utterly fearless.
Poor deluded visionary!
      He does not understand the ways of the world.
          But he is harmless.
Pilate returned to the bloodthirsty mob.
    "I have examined this man.
    I find no fault in him.
    He should be set free."
The mob roared displeasure at him.

      "Very well. Since he is a Galilean,
      take him to Herod!"

So they took Jesus to Herod.
      But the fox was wary.
          Quickly Herod satisfied his curiosity;
        This was no wonder-worker.
In mockery Herod robed Jesus
    in royal purple
        and returned him to Pilate.

AGAIN the problem was Pilate's
>and again he sought to avoid it.
>>"Whom should I release —
>>>Jesus or Barabbas?"
>>The Sanhedrin bloodlusters cried "Barabbas!"
>>and the crowd joined in.

"But the worst crime of Jesus
>is to call himself the King of the Jews."protested Pilate.

What?
>This meek mannered teacher of strange doctrines?
>This helpless prisoner of Rome?
>Him — king of the proud nation of Israel?

In fury the mob shouted:
>"Crucify Jesus! Release Barabbas!"
Pilate shrank back.
>He would have to quench their thirst for blood.
>"Scourge the prisoner!" he ordered.

The blood of the Master indeed flowed,
>as a brutal lash cut into his strong back
>>and his stainless brow was tortured
>>>with a crown of thorns.

WHEN Jesus stood before Pilate again,
    that beautiful sun-bronzed face was stained
        with his innocent blood.
Pilate's own pallid and indulgent features
    registered awe and admiration
        as he looked upon that magnificent specimen.
        His coarse lips trembled,
        and then cried:
        "Behold the man!"

SILENT to human ears
    a resounding echo
        thundered through the universe:

"Behold God and Man!"

AGHAST for a moment,
 the passionate mob flamed again,
 "Crucify him!"

Once more Pilate retreated
 to have a private audience with Jesus.
He feared this strange man
 and soon he returned again to ask the crowd to spare him.

But again they demanded the death of Jesus.

Pilate washed his soft hands
 in a silver basin.
  Protesting his own innocence
   he then surrendered the man he knew guiltless
    to the raging,
     mindless,
      murder-bent mob.

MOANING as some wounded beast
 a lone man makes his way
   out of the early morning sunshine
    into the shadows of the
     awful valley of Hinnon.

Stumbling among the dust and rocks
he fashions a noose for his neck
from the girdle of his coat.
  He ties the other end to a gnarled olive tree,
  and then hurls himself over the side of a cliff.

The knot holds but a moment,
  and the body of the doomed mortal
    tumbles through space
      and is broken on the rocks below.

  The terrible ravine is silent once more.

Pilgrims returning from the crucifixion
  would be surprised to discover
    thirty shining pieces of silver
      scattered over the floor of the temple.

THE early morning march of death
>> wound its way through the narrow streets
>>> of Jerusalem
>>> and just outside the gates
>>> Jesus fell,
>>>> pinned by the massive crossbeam of poplar.

It happened that a passing pilgrim
> Simon of Cyrene
>> was compelled to carry the heavy beam
>>> for the Creator Son of Nebadon
>>>> to the summit of the hill of horror.

> The intelligences of Nebadon
> gasped in shock
>> as cords cut sharply into the Master's flesh
>> and nails were driven into his hands and feet.
>> Even Lucifer turned his face away
>> as the bleeding Man of Peace
>> was lifted up to die between two thieves
>> under an ironic sign that read:
>> "Jesus of Nazareth — The King of the Jews."

THROUGH mists of pain Jesus saw his mother —
and there was Ruth! And Jude! And John!

    For a moment that wonderful smile flickered,
        and then faded.
    As the mob jeered Jesus,
        the soldiers cast lots for his tunic.

THE sky grew mysteriously dark;
the wind began to howl ominously.
Most of the crowd had sickened of its revenge
    and began to desert the barren hill of death.

Jesus scarcely noted when one of the thieves
        taunted him,
but when the other thief rebuked his brother criminal
    Jesus turned to look on him.
The poor man gazed into the dying eyes of the Prince
and pleaded in hoarse tones:
    "Jesus,
    Remember me when you come into your kingdom."

    The Master's words were a treasure to the
        redeemed soul:
    "You shall one day
    be with me in Paradise."

"MOTHER, behold your son!"

"John, behold your mother!"

"I desire for you to leave this place."

Now the sky was black.
Angry winds lashed with stinging sand
    at the huddled groups of people on the hill.

Barely heard above the moaning wind
was that wonderful, anguished voice of Jesus,
   reciting the cherished psalms of childhood
      as the specter of death relentlessly approached.

"I THIRST."

"It is finished!"

"Father, into your hands
   I commend my spirit!"

SLOWLY the noble head began to sink.

    Jesus closed his eyes
        to all the madness—
        all the pain—
        all the hate and darkness
            of Urantia.

That mighty heart stopped beating.

    Joshua ben Joseph,
    Jesus the Christ,
        was dead.

ABOVE the raging winds
the centurion's voice booms:

    "This was a righteous man!
    Truly he was a Son of God!"

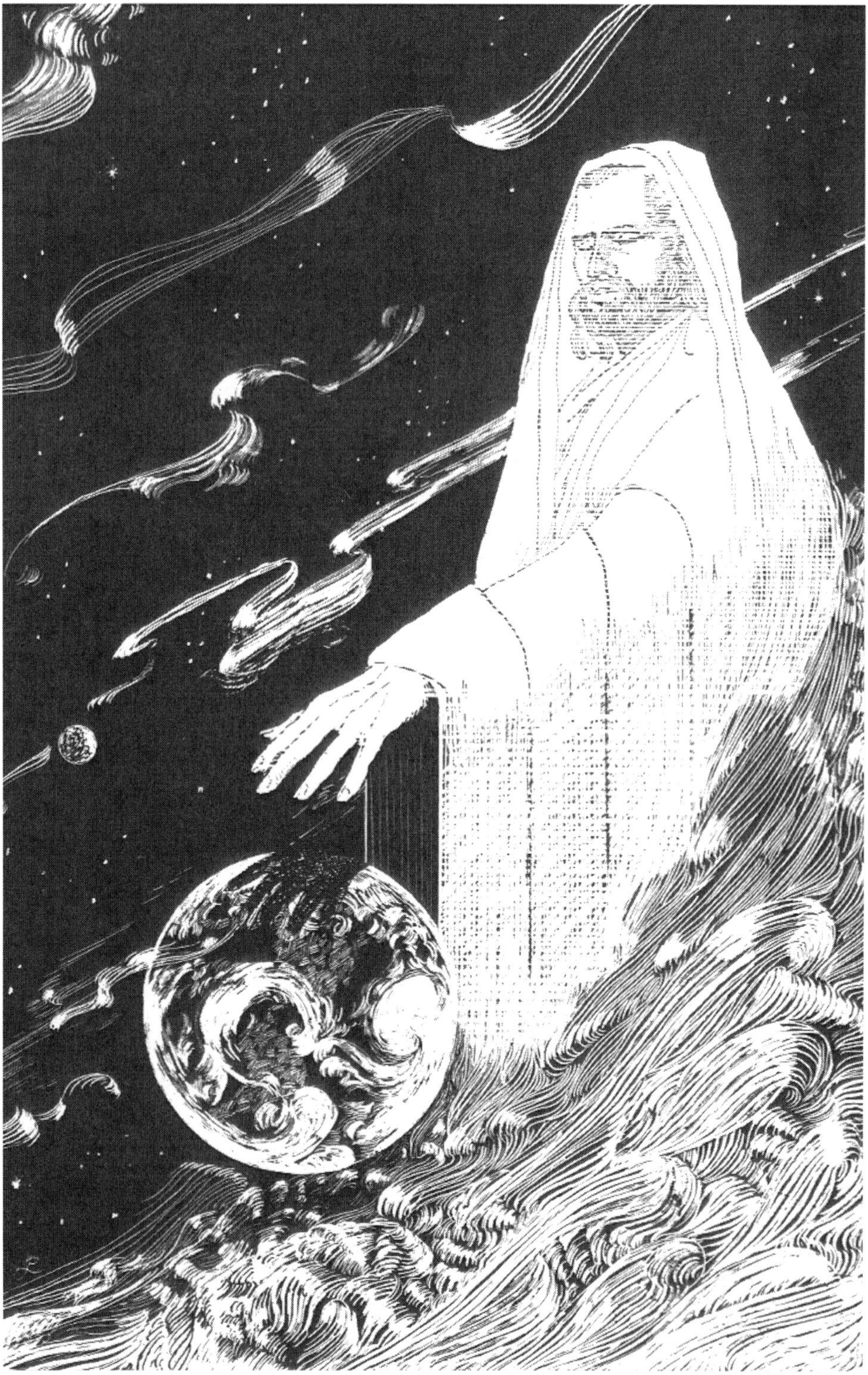

# JESUS:
God and Man

VII

" I will be with you, always."

THIS SUNDAY HAD BEEN A DAY OF RUMORS.

Alone in the Garden,
Peter tried to sort out his confusion.

"IF THE Master has risen," thought Peter,
"Why does he not come?
Perhaps I am no longer an apostle.
Perhaps I'm like Judas!
But the women said the Master told them
    'Go tell the apostles — and Peter!'"
Clenching his fists Peter cried,
    "I believe the Master has risen!"

The wonderful voice seemed to come from nowhere
and then Peter saw the figure before him.

"PETER — the enemy desired to take you in
    but I would not give you up!"

    The familiar, treasured tones of Jesus
        spoke to Peter of forgiveness and love
            and the awe-struck apostle listened
                until Jesus bade him farewell
                      and vanished in the mist.

BUT HIS brethren doubted the impetuous Peter,
    and none were satisfied until they had seen the Master.

Last to see Jesus was the disconsolate and despairing Thomas.
    When he beheld the risen Christ,
        he fell to his knees crying: "I believe, my Lord and Master."
            Jesus said to Thomas;
                "You have seen and heard Thomas, and you believe.
                Blessed are they in ages yet unborn
                who believe what they have not seen or heard."

DURING the season
    that the Master's Morontia form tarried
        he taught many lessons of faith to the
            apostles and other believers.

    But the time of Jesus of Nazareth
        and Michael on Urantia was nearly passed.

FOR THE last gathering
>the chosen mortals formed a ring of living faith
>>around the Creator Son.
>Below the mount of Olives the morning sunlight
>>streamed down on the doomed city of Jerusalem.

>Jesus spoke,
>bidding them await the
>Spirit of Truth —
>>the wondrous gift that would one day
>>enter any heart that dared make room for it.

"LOVE MEN even as I have loved you.
>Serve your fellow mortals
>>even as I have served you.
>By the spiritual fruits of your lives
>allure all men to the truth that we are all
>Sons and Daughters of God,
>and we are all brethren.
>Remember my teachings, and my life among you.
>My love overshadows you;
>My spirit will dwell with you;
>My peace shall abide with you.
>>>>>Farewell."
>The Master vanished from mortal eyes.

URANTIA was now called the
World of the Cross,
    the supreme symbol of Love and Service.
    Love transcendent over all;
    Love eternally creative;
    Love ever contagious.
        Nothing less than a new way of living;
        A path open to all.

AGAIN
a spiritual fragrance
descended upon Urantia
    and a refreshing wind
        permeated land and sea with
            the great gift of Michael of Nebadon:
            The Spirit of Truth.

TODAY the eternal message is unchanged:
Love, mercy, and ministry –
The Fatherhood of God,
and the Brotherhood of Man.

Jesus is forever: God and Man!

"MY LOVE overshadows you;

> My spirit dwells with you;
> My peace abides upon you;
> I will go with you into the world;
> I will not forsake you.
>
> I am with you, Always!"

Manufactured by Amazon.ca
Acheson, AB